Growing Older as a Trans and/or Non-Binary Person

by the same author

Supporting Transgender and Non-Binary People with Disabilities or Illnesses
A Good Practice Guide for Health and Care Provision
Jennie Kermode
ISBN 978 1 78592 541 2
eISBN 978 1 78450 935 4

Transgender Employees in the Workplace
A Guide for Employers
Jennie Kermode
ISBN 978 1 78592 228 2
eISBN 978 1 78450 544 8

of related interest

Lesbian, Gay, Bisexual and Transgender Ageing
Biographical Approaches for Inclusive Care and Support
Edited by Richard Ward, Ian Rivers and Mike Sutherland
ISBN 978 1 84905 257 3
eISBN 978 1 85700 537 3

Transgender Health
A Practitioner's Guide to Binary and Non-Binary Trans Patient Care
Ben Vincent, PhD
ISBN 978 1 78592 201 5
eISBN 978 1 78450 475 5

Theorizing Transgender Identity for Clinical Practice
A New Model for Understanding Gender
S.J. Langer
ISBN 978 1 78592 765 2
eISBN 978 1 78450 642 1

Growing Older as a Trans and/or Non-Binary Person

A Support Guide

Jennie Kermode

Jessica Kingsley Publishers
London and Philadelphia

First published in Great Britain in 2021 by Jessica Kingsley Publishers
An Hachette Company

2

Front cover image source: Anna Bliokh/iStock.

The information contained in this book is not intended to replace the services
of trained medical professionals or to be a substitute for medical advice. You
are advised to consult a doctor on any matters relating to your health, and in
particular on any matters that may require diagnosis or medical attention.

A CIP catalogue record for this title is available from the
British Library and the Library of Congress

ISBN 978 1 78775 363 1
eISBN 978 1 78775 364 8

Printed and bound in Great Britain by Clays Ltd

Jessica Kingsley Publishers' policy is to use papers that are natural,
renewable and recyclable products and made from wood grown in
sustainable forests. The logging and manufacturing processes are expected
to conform to the environmental regulations of the country of origin.

Jessica Kingsley Publishers
Carmelite House
50 Victoria Embankment
London EC4Y 0DZ

www.jkp.com

For Colleen, who never had the chance to get old.

Contents

Acknowledgements

It would not have been possible to produce this book without the older trans people who volunteered to discuss their experiences and share their insights. Some agreed to be quoted, and they are referred to here by their first names only, in order to protect their privacy.

Introduction

Despite what stories in the media might make you think, being transgender (trans) is not a new phenomenon. We can find stories of gender-nonconforming people throughout recorded history, and many myths and legends explore the desire to transform the body accordingly. It has only been possible to do this using modern surgical or hormonal techniques for around a century, in a process which has been constantly improving. Because its pioneers were very few in number, and people didn't really start transitioning this way in significant numbers until the 1990s, we haven't really had many elderly transitioned people in society – until now.

This doesn't mean that we haven't had older trans people getting by without treatment. The difference is that fewer of them have been visible in society. It has been easier for them to conceal their difference for safety reasons. The fewer people who came out of the closet, the stranger they seemed to others, often attracting higher levels of hostility and certainly finding it harder to go about their day-to-day lives. It has taken a big movement of people coming out, raising awareness and supporting each other to get to where we are today.

Other factors complicate this picture. We know that rates of mental illness and suicidal ideation are higher among trans people who lack the opportunity to transition, so it's probable that fewer trans people made it to old age. Additionally, lower levels of awareness in society at large (at least in Europe) meant that trans people themselves also lacked a conceptual framework or a language through which to make sense of their feelings. In recent years, a number of very elderly trans people have spoken publicly about always knowing they were different but not knowing how, or not knowing what they could do about it.

The consequence of all this is that it's only very recently that our society has started to think about the needs of older trans people and how we might best provide for them. Very little research has been done directly in this area and very little written on this subject. This book is based on multiple interviews with older trans people and with trans people who are just reaching the point in life where they're starting to plan for their old age. They're working out how to navigate systems around pensions, health and social care, wills and inheritance that were not designed with them in mind. They're experiencing the bodily changes that happen to everyone with age, but without a clear map of what's likely to happen. They're also discovering the joys of getting older and becoming more confident and more at ease with the world around them.

There's no one-size-fits-all model for older people. Everyone's experience is different. What this book seeks to do is to explore the experiences that many trans and non-binary people have in common, and look at the areas where these differ from the experiences of others.

If you are trans or non-binary, this book can help you to make sense of your experiences, anticipate problems and recognise that, no matter how you may feel, you're not alone in dealing with these challenges. It may help you to get more out of your golden years.

If you work for an organisation that supports older people, this book can help you to provide an inclusive service which is better at providing for trans and non-binary people. It provides examples of best practice, suggests ways to resolve common difficulties, and aims to help you better relate to the people you're working with.

A note on style

Throughout this book, the pronouns they/them/their are used in the singular form when referencing non-binary individuals or hypothetical individuals whose gender is undetermined. Although the author recognises that some people consider this to be poor English, its utility in this context is undeniable. Despite what many people think, it is not a new phenomenon; in fact, the earliest recorded uses of singular *they* as a gender-neutral pronoun date back to the 14th century.[1]

1

Experiences of Being Trans or Non-Binary

Ordinarily, when you open a book like this, you might expect a preface explaining what it means to be trans or non-binary so that readers without personal experience of that can get up to speed. In this case, the picture is a little more complicated because social understanding of these things has changed over time, as have the ways in which trans and non-binary people perceive and understand themselves. In order to connect with these different experiences, it helps to start with a little bit of history.

At its broadest, the term *trans* is used to describe everybody whose experience of their own gender – their personal sense of whether they are male, female or something else – is different from what was expected of them when they were born. Within this there is a wide range of different experiences and ways of living. These emerge not just from trans people themselves but from the ways they interact with the world around them, which varies depending on social and cultural factors. Because our society and our cultures have changed a lot over the past few decades, it's important to understand a bit about these changes in order to better understand how older trans people feel about gender and how that might have changed over the course of their lives.

Trans pioneers

There have always been trans people, but not every society has recognised their existence or perceived them in the way that we do today. Since the Christianisation of Europe, most European societies – and those societies elsewhere established, conquered or heavily influenced by European settlers – have recognised only two genders, male and female, defined in most instances by bodily appearance at birth. Towards the end of the 1800s, some sections of Western society began to query this model, partly due to increased academic acknowledgement of homosexuality,[2] which was frequently confused with gender variance.

In North America, there was a growing recognition that indigenous peoples used several different gender systems, and these models, existing in parallel with those used by white people, prompted individuals in the latter group who felt uncomfortable about their own assigned gender – as well as doctors, scientists and philosophers with an interest in the subject – to wonder if there might be alternative ways that *they* could understand gender. There was also increased awareness of intersex people throughout Western society. Previously dismissed as freaks, and often persecuted, they became the subject of a new scientific interest in the complexity of biological sex (often at the price of great suffering to them as individuals), which in turn prompted curiosity about gender. In fact, most intersex people are cisgender, but this was not well understood by those in positions of influence at the time.

Adding to these factors was the influence of the wars that took place during this period. Advancements in medical technology meant that wounded soldiers were far more likely to be evacuated from the battlefield and treated, while a new focus on hygiene meant that this would frequently involve undressing and washing them. As a consequence, it was discovered that significant numbers of people raised as female were presenting themselves as men in order to go and fight. We should be wary of assuming that all these people were trans as they could have had other reasons for doing what they did, such as a desire to serve their countries, make money or avenge fallen relatives, but some certainly were, and the discovery prompted public conversations about what it meant to be male or female.

Although she was far from the first person to undergo a surgically supported transition, the woman who first brought transness to widespread public attention was Christine Jorgensen, who became famous after being featured in a *New York Daily News* story.[3] Naturally suited to celebrity, she worked as an actress and singer, and talked extensively about her treatment (which included the pioneering use of oestrogen) and how happy she was with her new life. Her story made the international press, and for many trans people in the UK it provided the first glimmer of hope that it might be possible to overcome dysphoria completely.

Transsexual or transgender?

The term *transsexual* first entered the English language in 1949 and was initially used quite loosely to refer to trans people with various different ways of understanding and expressing their gender. In 1960, the influential US magazine *Transvestia*, under the editorship of Virginia Prince, sought to standardise language use among trans people themselves and advanced the term *transgender* as a label for trans women who were attracted to women and did not wish to have transition-related surgery. Prince was personally invested in distinguishing people in this situation from those who wished to physically transition because she had lost her marriage as a result of the way she presented herself, and she felt that she could normalise people like herself in the eyes of the public if only she could disassociate them from those who attracted the most intense forms of prejudice. At the time, the public in the US (and UK) had little awareness of trans people, but homophobia was entrenched. Prince's contention was that female-attracted trans women who didn't have surgery were engaging in healthy self-expression (with nothing as controversial about it as altering the body) and were nothing to do with male-attracted trans women, whom the public perceived as homosexual.

Although Prince's position was controversial even at the time, her use of language stuck, with the term *transgender* extended over time so that it also included trans men who didn't have surgery. There were two key reasons for this. First, many people were ready to use any available term to try to defend themselves from a society that frequently challenged the validity of their experiences and completely misrepresented them. Second, the distinction appealed to many people who were proud to transition surgically, and who happily described themselves as transsexual. Some of them felt that their transition demonstrated their commitment to their gender and therefore proved its validity, and argued that it was those who didn't have surgery who were perverted or were exploiting their situation in order to indulge trivial desires.

In 1996, the situation changed again with the publication of Leslie Feinberg's influential book *Transgender Warriors: Making History from Joan of Arc to Dennis Rodman*,[4] which argued that *transgender* should be used to refer to all trans people. It was adopted as an umbrella term by most major Scottish LGBT (lesbian, gay, bisexual, transgender) organisations the following year, and by the end of the century there was substantial support for it across the UK, with numerous community projects using *transgender* either as their term of preference or as an umbrella term, acknowledging the use of other, more specific terms alongside it.

The term *transsexual* decreased in popularity for two reasons. Some people felt that it was problematic because it created confusion between gender and sexuality, which was additionally unfortunate because the media had a history of implying that being trans was a sexual fetish and that trans people were likely to be sex offenders. Others contended that it perpetuated the idea that being trans was centred on undergoing a process of change, which didn't reflect the experiences of the majority of trans people. The idea that trans people are 'born in the wrong bodies' has traditionally been used as a simplified way of explaining trans experiences to cis people, and relatively few trans people think of themselves in that way.

By 2012, the majority of trans people preferred to describe themselves as transgender, regardless of their sexual orientation or surgical status, and *transsexual* continued to be used only by a small group of people, most of whom had come out or transitioned before 2000. Other older people adopted the same term as the younger generation.

If you work with older trans people, you need to be aware that they may use either term and may have strong feelings about it, potentially taking offence if they are described using the other. Because this is a sensitive issue and many trans people have had to fight hard to have any control over the language used to describe them, it's important to show respect and use each individual's preferred term.

The transgender umbrella, trans* and trans

As noted above, it was during the early 21st century that the term *transgender umbrella* came into common parlance. The idea was to use the term *transgender* to cover a variety of different identities including transsexual people, non-binary people and transvestites/cross-dressers (who sometimes describe themselves as non-binary but often don't). Intersex people were sometimes included as well, until intersex organisations made it clear that they did not consider this to be appropriate.

The idea of using *transgender* in this way was that it would make it easier for individuals and organisations to refer collectively to people who experienced similar kinds of prejudice and discrimination. Some people objected to it because they felt that the groups it covered were too different. In some cases, they argued that advocating on behalf of one group covered by the umbrella could disadvantage another. Over time, most people adjusted to the idea, but it still has critics, especially among older demographics.

Over time, *transgender* began to be shortened to *trans* in day-to-day speech, enabling people to talk about *trans men*, *trans women*, *trans people*, etc. (*trans* is an adjective so the space in each of these terms is important, just as it would be if you were talking about fat men or happy women). Many people began to add an asterisk – *trans** – in order to stress that they were using the term inclusively – that is, for everyone under the transgender umbrella or everyone who self-identified as trans. In recent years, however, use of the asterisk has declined due to a growing belief within the communities concerned that *trans* should always be used inclusively, and therefore interpreted as inclusive, unless otherwise specified.

2

Changing Ideas about Gender

Just as ideas about what it means to be transgender have changed over the years, so have ideas about what it means to be male or female, masculine or feminine. This adds to the risk of communication difficulties between older trans or non-binary people and their younger family members or service providers they may need to interact with, and it can compound the sense of not really being understood that many older people experience.

Growing up trans in the mid-20th century

In the 1940s, 1950s and 1960s, children in the UK were raised from birth with very different expectations of life, based on their gender. Although it was becoming commonplace for women to be in paid employment for at least part of their lives, they earned substantially less than men, and it was generally expected that men would be the breadwinners while women would stay at home and care for children. This manifested early on with girls being given dolls, dolls' houses and toys reflecting domestic tasks (such as miniature tea sets) to play with, while boys were encouraged to play with more physical activity-focused toys and to engage in outdoor games with their peers. Girls were taught to do housework (including tasks such as sewing which are now less frequently taught), while boys were encouraged to take on responsibility and prepare for a future as heads of their own households. They often began working or became apprentices while still in their mid-teens.

In Scotland and Wales, most schools were mixed-sex, but in England the majority of children attended either a boys' school or a girls' school throughout this period. It was rare (though by no means impossible) for girls to go on to higher education, and jokes about them doing so only as a means of finding husbands reflected a deep-rooted belief that they were unlikely to take careers seriously.

Sports and social groups for children were almost all segregated by sex during this period, and boys and girls generally only got the chance to play together if they were related or were taking part in wider community events. As a consequence, although feminists persisted in campaigning for adult women to have more of the same opportunities as men, it was easy for children to believe that there was a great gulf between the experiences and abilities of boys and girls.

This separation of roles and physical spaces made life very difficult for trans and non-binary children. Behaviour that didn't fit with gendered expectations immediately drew attention. Punishment for such behaviour was frequently violent and gave those children who didn't fit in a deep sense of fear and shame. Parents were discouraged from turning a blind eye and were warned that allowing their children to ignore gender conventions could result in them becoming homosexual (and therefore, in the case of those raised as boys, criminal).

Compounding this was a social tendency to try to protect girls and women by restricting their behaviour. Female-assigned people who displayed masculine behaviours – such as wearing trousers or smoking cigarettes – were seen as troublemakers and found it harder to get taken seriously if they were the victims of male sexual aggression. As a result, trans men growing up during this period were significantly less likely than those born later in the century to present in masculine ways early in life. Many would go on to take refuge in feminist spaces or lesbian spaces, regardless of their politics or sexual orientation, until it eventually became easier for them to express who they were within mainstream society.

Despite all these challenges, some trans people managed to find supportive and understanding doctors during this period, and accessed a variety of medical procedures including hormone treatment and surgery. Despite what younger people might expect, some retain a degree of nostalgia for this period because they feel they got a lot of individual attention and carefully considered, personally tailored treatment. They fear that today people presenting with similar symptoms are categorised too quickly and may actually find it harder to get exactly what they need. Others, however, feel that they were forced to present an extreme version of their actual gender in order to access any treatment at all, and that this was damaging.

Growing up trans in the late 20th century

The impact of second-wave feminism on public ideas about gender in the late 20th century saw a shift in parental behaviours that enabled a generation of children to grow up with less strictly enforced gender roles and expectations.[5] Alongside pink and blue, babies wore yellow, lilac and white, and nurseries were frequently decorated in these more socially neutral colours. In most households, boys and girls were permitted to play with most of the same toys, although wheeled toys were less likely to be given to girls and there was still a taboo against boys playing with dolls. Young children were also dressed in similar ways. Trousers and dungarees were common on girls, as was short hair. Boys often had mid-length haircuts, although these became less common over the years. This meant that there was some room for children to express their gender ambiguously if doing so felt more comfortable for them.

In schools during this period, children generally studied together but were often divided into boys and girls for convenience during classroom activities, and physical activities were frequently segregated, even for quite young children, with sports like football and rugby available to boys only whereas netball and hockey were the sole preserve of girls. Strict gender roles were enforced during classes in dancing. In secondary education, girls were encouraged to take classes in home economics while boys were encouraged to study woodwork or metalwork. Rules about who could participate in such classes relaxed over time, but social taboos took longer to disappear. Some women who were school pupils during this period also report that they were actively discouraged by teachers from studying maths or science, which were thought of as boys' subjects. There was a general belief that girls would not be as capable in these areas.

Most social organisations serving children at this time were gender-segregated. In general, boys were expected to socialise with boys, and girls with girls, but this was not particularly strictly enforced and mixed-sex social groups were fairly commonplace.

The 1970s saw a substantial wave of immigration from Commonwealth countries in response to a labour shortage, resulting in the formation or expansion of immigrant communities which, partly as a consequence of other people's prejudice and partly for linguistic and cultural reasons, were often quite inwardly focused. Those who grew up in such communities during this period report that they were held to strict behavioural standards due to a fear that any bad behaviour on their part would reflect badly on the whole community and potentially increase the hostility it faced. This was a particularly difficult situation for children who found it hard to fit into prescribed gender roles.

Although efforts at integration and making a good impression had a positive impact on the lives of many girls who came from backgrounds where, traditionally, they would not have had as many opportunities, there was a concomitant attempt to adopt British attitudes to gender and sexuality which created prejudice in communities that would traditionally have been more accepting. Although there is some evidence of a gradual relaxation of attitudes in line with wider society, trans people from minority immigrant communities continue to face these difficulties to this day.

The introduction of Clause 28 (Section 2A in Scotland) in 1988 expressly forbade 'the teaching of homosexuality as a pretend family relationship'. It emerged from an increasingly intense campaign of newspaper hostility towards gay people, starting in the early 1980s and feeding off the widespread social panic about AIDS. The result of all this was to create a climate of fear, hostility and ignorance,[6] even among children. As anybody breaking gender-related taboos was first and foremost assumed to be gay, this exposed young trans people to a significant risk of peer aggression. Children learned early on that they had to conform. It was not uncommon for trans teenagers to go to extremes of gendered behaviour in the roles assigned to them in order to try to conceal – or somehow overcome – their underlying feelings about who they were. As a rule, young people had no option to adopt openly LGBT identities until they moved out of the parental home, and even then there was a tendency to be circumspect about where and with whom they expressed them.

Gender roles for children today

Most older trans people share the view that despite the increasing availability of young trans role models and increasing social acceptance of gender variance in the early 21st century, most children today find themselves faced with stricter gender expectations than their parents and grandparents did. The introduction of the gender reveal party – recently criticised by its inventor,[7] who says she now knows better – encourages parents to start thinking in strictly gendered terms before their children are even born, and to share that experience with their friends and relatives, who will then buy them the clothes, toys and other gifts they associate with boys or with girls. The notion that boys should be in blue and girls in pink (a complete reversal from Victorian times when pink, being a pale version of red, was thought too strong a colour for girls) has returned with a vengeance and is intensely present in the marketing of baby products.

This polarised approach to gender means that there's less and less space, at least in the social mainstream, for children to experiment with different ways of expressing their gender. Unless they directly assert the fact that they want to express their gender in a non-standard way – which may or may not receive support – there is little middle ground between presenting as a boy or a girl.

At the same time as this has happened, a counter-trend has emerged which supports gender ambiguity in children for the sake of exploration and play. It's important to note that this option isn't something all parents feel is available to them, with some sections of society intensely hostile towards it, but schools are increasingly accepting of gender-ambivalent children. The difference between this and the ambiguity of expression available to children in the late 20th century is that it allows for a conscious decision to cross gender boundaries, rather than enforcing a strict binary system that nevertheless allowed children to express aspects of their gender in an androgynous way without really standing out.

As a result of these changes, it can be difficult for today's generation of parents – and those who don't have children of their own but are alert to the debate going on around other people's – to appreciate how different things were for their parents and grandparents. Today, young trans and non-binary people tend to be much more aware of the way their gender experience fits into society, so that as they grow up, they realise what their options are. They also (usually) have the internet available to them as a source of information, and far more access to relevant support groups. It's important for younger adults to recognise that this awareness and these resources were not available to older trans people at that stage in life, with the result that they understood themselves and related to society in very different ways. The effects of that different experience have in many cases remained throughout their lives.

'I think of the impossibility I had, when I first came out as trans, of coming out as a non-binary person,' says Jo, 'because non-binary people didn't exist, just as, when I was a child, trans people didn't exist. And so there's been this, for me, constant struggle to assert myself and then to understand that actually, you know, it's all right these days. I don't have to hide myself the way I always used to have to.'

Growing up non-binary in the 20th century

Despite the fact that there has been some mainstream recognition of the existence of binary transgender people since the early 20th century, it's only really been in this century that Western society has begun to acknowledge the existence of non-binary people to any significant degree. This means that older non-binary people are more likely to have struggled to find positive ways of identifying themselves when growing up. Some tried to make the best of life in their assigned gender roles, while others went through a binary transition process with results that didn't fully satisfy them or resolve their dysphoria. Some went through a belated coming-out process – or a second coming-out process – when non-binary identities became an option for them. Some are keen to stress that they were always aware of where their identity lay, even if they didn't have words with which to describe it or didn't feel that anybody else would understand what they were trying to say.

The fact that non-binary identities have only recently emerged into the spotlight means that some people perceive them as a modern fad, but there have always been non-binary people (as the recognition of more than two genders in numerous other cultures demonstrates) and it did not prove difficult to find older non-binary people when researching this book, including people who are open about their gender with those around them.

The impact of sexism

The experience of going through life as a trans person is also impacted by the differing opportunities that society offers to adult men and women, which is also something that has changed considerably over the past few decades. Perhaps the most dramatic illustration of this lies in the difference between the number of trans men and the number of trans women choosing to transition. Although those numbers are now evening out, until the start of this century the number of transitioned trans women vastly outweighed that of trans men.

Each group faced a different set of barriers. Because they began life in male roles, trans women were more likely to be financially independent and less likely to be primary carers for children or older relatives, both of which made it easier for them to shape their own lives. A feminine person originally categorised as male was, however, much more easily identified. A masculine person raised as female could exist more discreetly within society, at least from the 1970s onwards, when it ceased to be unusual for women to wear trousers and have short hair. Trans men living in this way could still be subject to hostility and discrimination, but they faced a lesser degree of moral outrage because their gender variance usually went unrecognised and it was assumed instead that they were making a political statement. This meant that although it was more of a struggle for them to get their gender taken seriously, they could live their lives in a relatively natural way without coming out, whereas trans women had a choice between living as men, being socially ostracised, transitioning (where possible) to the point where they could 'pass' as cis women, or seeking safety in marginalised communities where they were accepted. (A few brave individuals from both these groups, of course, faced their challengers head on and won the respect of their wider communities against the odds.)

The different value that society places on men and women means that people perceived as women who behave in a masculine way have traditionally been seen as gaining something, whereas people perceived as men who behave in a feminine way have been seen as losing something. Hostility to trans men has generally been centred on this idea that they are overreaching themselves and need to be put back in their place, whereas hostility to trans women has been centred on the idea that they are behaving in an inexplicable way and that they must therefore have hidden motives. Because women are seen as sexual objects, these motives are often assumed to be sexual. Trans women also risk being accused of trying to shirk male responsibilities, although this argument is less common now that a broader range of opportunities is available to women (for instance, in the military). Both groups face a risk of sexual violence as a result.

Non-binary people pose a more explicit challenge to the established social order. Many go under the radar – even if they would prefer not to – whereas others are in a position of being permanently visible as gender variant, and subject to the kind of prejudices described above, with the difference that today transfeminine non-binary people, as well as transmasculine ones, are often perceived as political – something that was not the case in the last century. In parts of society where trans men and trans women gradually became more accepted, progress for non-binary people was slower. They are often perceived (including by trans people) as less genuine than binary trans people, partly due to an assumption that a person's level of dysphoria was directly correlated with the degree of change that person needed to make to their presentation or body (something that is not borne out by the testimony of non-binary people themselves, some of whom experience severe dysphoria if forced to live as male or female). They encounter some similar kinds of prejudice to those faced by bisexual people, with the assumption being that they have a choice about how to live, whereas binary trans people 'can't help it' – a myth which is additionally problematic because it implies that even if binary trans people should be accepted, it is only out of pity, and that any kind of transition – or, by implication, deviation from approved binary sex roles – is a moral failing.

Conversion therapy

During the mid-20th century, trans people who opened up about their gender when they were still young were significantly more likely than they are today to meet with hostile reactions. Some were rejected outright by their families, going to stay with more distant relatives, going into the foster system or ending up on the streets. Some remained with their families but were subjected to attempts to beat their difference out of them. Others were subjected to various forms of what is referred to today as *conversion therapy*.

Conversion therapy could be as simple as going to see a counsellor or psychoanalyst to talk through suspected underlying issues, although this should not be assumed to be a benign form of treatment, as patients often felt that they were subjected to intense psychological pressure or encouraged to doubt their own sanity to a degree that made it difficult for them to function in normal life thereafter. In other cases, patients were told to follow a recommended therapeutic regime involving the pursuit of what were considered to be more appropriately gendered activities. At the more extreme end, they could be subjected to electroshock therapy.

Outside the purview of mainstream psychiatry, conversion therapy was also practised by some religious groups. Although there is evidence that this remains the case today, it now appears to be significantly less common. This type of therapy could, again, be focused on talking, usually with an additional element of prayer and ritual cleansing. It could also involve group rituals up to and including exorcism in situations where being trans was interpreted by a community as a form of possession by malignant spirits. Trans people who have been through rituals like this report them as intensely traumatic.

Where such procedures were carried out against the trans person's will, there was often an additional feeling of having been betrayed by family or community members who let them happen. Where trans people consented, they sometimes suffered feelings of guilt about their own complicity, which further complicated their trauma.

It's important to recognise that conversion therapy was not something that trans people always resisted. Indeed, some sought it out themselves rather than being forced to undergo it. They often tried very hard to change, recognising that doing so would make their lives much easier. There is no evidence, however, that conversion therapy has ever been effective in changing somebody's experience of gender.

The psychological damage done by conversion therapy can last a lifetime. Many older trans people (and some younger ones) have mental health problems associated with experiences of this sort, and even if these are not apparent all the time, they can lead to intense feelings of fear, anger or lack of self-worth when something prompts memories of the treatment to return.

The social cost of transition

Alongside conversion therapy and straight-out violence, throughout the mid- and late 20th century other forms of pressure were exerted on trans people to keep them from transitioning. Although these pressures still exist in the UK today, especially within certain minority communities, there are now a sufficient number of prominent counter-narratives that they no longer hold the power that they once did.

Trans people growing up during this period were frequently told that they would never be sexually desirable, that nobody would ever love them, that they would never marry and that they would never have children. Adopting children as an openly trans person was not an option until the 21st century, and in the event that a marriage broke up due to a trans person coming out, custody of any children would almost always go to the cis partner, with the trans partner frequently being denied any access at all. Because trans people were vulnerable to blackmail over access to their children and because they often felt that they needed to cling on to the relationships they had because they would never find others, they faced an elevated risk of domestic abuse.

It was very difficult for visibly trans people to get work in mainstream industries, which meant that many experienced long periods of unemployment or ended up working in the sex industry. They also faced significant discrimination when attempting to rent private accommodation, and it was not uncommon for them to be denied service in shops and restaurants, all of which was completely legal. Police harassment was not uncommon, and trans people who ended up in the prison system (which, at one stage, could happen simply because of how they were dressed) were routinely placed in prisons associated with the gender they were identified as at birth, which makes trans women and transfeminine non-binary people highly vulnerable to sexual violence.[8]

Numerous studies have shown that prejudice and discrimination contribute to suicidal ideation[9] and self-harm[10] in trans people. It's impossible to know what happened to trans people who grew up during this period and never felt able to come out, but rates of depression and anxiety are high in the trans population and many older trans people report having experienced severe mental health problems during the course of their lives. Isolation seems to be particularly damaging, and finding supportive communities makes a big positive difference, which is why it's very important for trans people to be able to stay in touch with their communities as they get older and to be able to find new supportive environments if their circumstances change.

3

Gender – a Modern Understanding

Today ideas about gender are much more clearly formulated. Although there are ongoing debates around what is biological and what is social in origin, as well as continuing arguments over language and semantics, most specialists agree on the basics of gender as it is experienced.

Less precise is the way we commonly talk about gender. The term has two broadly accepted meanings, which don't always fit together very well.

First, there is gender as a social construct – a way of thinking that we use for organisational purposes in day-to-day life. This involves people being expected to fit into certain social roles and exhibit certain behaviours based on how they or other people identify their gender. In the UK, it means that women are generally expected to be caring and empathetic, good at compromising, concerned about their appearance and fond of children, whereas men are expected to be independent, emotionally resilient, assertive, logical and protective of their families. These stereotypes, which encompass many other characteristics and behaviours, can be very limiting and have significant real-world consequences across everything from employment to personal safety. As a consequence, many people reject them. This accounts for instances of hostility towards trans people, who are sometimes perceived (in most cases incorrectly) as being keen to perpetuate them (the idea being that they transition because they associate their instinctive characteristics or behaviours with a gender role different to the one in which they were raised).

Second, there is gender as an aspect of identity. This involves the internal feeling of being male, female or something else. Experts are divided on whether it is something inborn[11] or something that develops early in life, but they no longer consider a gender that doesn't match what's expected for a particular body type to be a mental illness.[12] Just to complicate things, the strength of this internal sense of gender seems to vary from one person to another. Some cisgender people assert, for instance, that, aside from initial surprise and social inconvenience, it really wouldn't bother them if they discovered that their sex characteristics had changed, and this reflects the experience of some trans people who feel that they are living in the wrong gender category but don't experience much distress as a result. (As noted earlier, this variation in strength of feeling doesn't seem to correlate to any particular gender – it's possible to have a strong sense of being non-binary.)

Although trans people can run into difficulties because of the social construct of gender, just like anyone else, it's the internal experience that really makes their lives difficult. This is why, for most trans people, expanding popular notions of what each gender category can include, or even doing away with social gender altogether, won't make it possible to live comfortably without undergoing any physical changes. There certainly are trans people who are able to live happily without surgery or hormones as long as their gender is respected by those around them, but others find that their quality of life is significantly improved by medical intervention.

People who disagree with the medical consensus and perceive transness as a product of the imagination or an ideological fad often contend that if the mind and body appear to be out of alignment, it's the mind that ought to be changed. There have, however, been many attempts to change trans people's sense of gender over the past century, often with willing trans participants, and there is no evidence of any having succeeded. What has been noted is that such attempts increase the risk of suicidal ideation and self-harm in the person treated,[13] as a result of which an increasing number of countries are clamping down on them.[14]

Keeping up with changing ideas

If you have grown up with a gender that matches what society expects for you, you will always have had a map of sorts to guide you through life. Society's changing ideas about gender may have opened up unexpected opportunities, but it's unlikely that you have been faced with anything like as many changes as trans people have faced during the same period. There were no useful maps for older trans people, and many have struggled to keep track of changes that affect how they are perceived but may not have directly impacted their lives in ways they're aware of.

Language, in particular, changes all the time, and it can be bewildering. This isn't just an issue for outsiders – older trans people often struggle to keep up with the variety of terms that younger people are using to describe or express their gender. The thing to bear in mind is that until fairly recently it has been impossible to have wide-ranging open discussions about trans experiences, so language has a lot of catching up to do. The chances are that people have always had these varied experiences but have lacked the words with which to describe them. Based on what we can observe about language change in other areas, it seems likely that the number of terms will be reduced over time as a gradual consensus is reached and some of those that mean roughly the same thing drop out of use.

Individual trans people are often expected to be experts on all things trans and so feeling out of touch due to language change can be frustrating. This is, however, probably an inevitable effect of society becoming more accepting, and a precursor to more people recognising that trans people are as different from one another as members of any other group. Even if the new language sounds quirky and faddish, the ideas it's being used to discuss may be valuable. Some older people who have had fixed ways of explaining their gender for a long time are gradually starting to adopt new terms themselves and find that it helps them to talk about how they feel in a more nuanced way, even if not everyone can understand and share in those conversations.

Changing scientific ideas about transness can also present challenges. Many people are excited by the search for a genetic or neurological cause of being trans, but others worry that this could lead to new efforts to 'cure' them when they're happy about who they are, or fear that it could lead to the selective abortion of trans foetuses. Still others think that it's beside the point and that they shouldn't have to look to biology to justify their identity because they're doing no harm by living as they do. Most trans people welcomed transness ceasing to be classified as a mental illness, but others worried that it could make it harder to access treatment, and some people still wish that there was a way for them to live happily in their birth gender – or at least to have that choice.

'I don't think the trans label ever really fitted me because of all of the garbage that goes around it,' says Eleanor, who finds herself at odds with the present consensus over several issues. 'It's a useful model, and that's it.' She finds that the most straightforward way to describe herself is simply as gender dysphoric, and regards it as problematic that people with non-standard experiences of gender are expected to share the same political or philosophical beliefs when there's really no reason why they would do so.

It's important for those who support and work with older trans people to recognise this diversity of ideas and opinions, and not expect them to be homogeneous. Trans people no more share a single way of thinking than, say, all cis women do. It's not uncommon for older trans people to come into conflict with younger ones who perceive them as transphobic because they don't share more recent ideas about trans issues, but this doesn't mean that one group is any more or less genuine in its experience or intent than the other.

Gender identification at birth

The vast majority of people are allotted to one gender category or the other at birth on the basis of a simple glance at the genitals. For some it's more complicated, with clearly ambiguous anatomy leading to further testing and potentially to surgical intervention in an attempt to make the child fit more neatly into one of these categories, something that many intersex adults strongly object to.[15] Although the majority of people born with penises will go through life comfortably identifying as male and the majority of those born with vaginas will identify as female, neither simple assignment nor intervention provides any guarantee that an individual will fit this pattern.

The consensus today is that children usually develop a sense of gender between the ages of three and seven.[16] This applies regardless of whether or not their gender conflicts with other people's expectations based on their anatomy.[17] At the time of writing, there is no provision in law in any part of the UK for a change of gender on official documents before a person reaches the age of 18, but many people now undergo a social transition at an earlier age. Although there are isolated examples of children socially transitioning throughout history, and although similar lifestyle changes have been widely practised in some other cultures[18] (for a variety of reasons), this was not generally considered an option for children growing up in the UK over most of the past century.

As a result of these changes in the way we think about gender at birth and in childhood, there is quite a bit of variability in the way that older trans people think about their identities over the life course. Some feel that their gender was always as it is today, whereas others feel strongly that they became men or women only after transition (it is rare for non-binary people to adopt an equivalent position). Some older trans and non-binary people feel that the experience of being trans is something that belongs to adulthood, and that it's inappropriate for children to undergo any type of transition. This is sometimes (though not exclusively) related to their belief that trans experiences are connected with sexuality, or to a worry that other people making that assumption could place children exploring their gender at risk.

Gender and sexual orientation

Most people now agree that gender is quite separate from sexual orientation. To put it simply, sexual orientation is about who you are attracted to and gender is about who you *are*. Transgender people have the same range of sexual orientations as the general population. Despite what is sometimes claimed, there is no evidence that anyone transitioning in the UK today does so in order to 'become straight' – that is, to live in a gender role different from that of the people they're attracted to. Indeed, as the evidence suggests that transphobia is more widespread than homophobia in the UK today,[19] there would seem to be little to gain from doing this, at least in mainstream communities.

For older people who have grown up around a different set of beliefs, however, distinguishing gender and sexual orientation can be more difficult. Within the gay community, there's a long-standing tradition of dressing in drag or adopting stereotypical feminine behaviours as a means of expressing one's desire to interact with men as a woman might be expected to. Some older gay men express themselves in this way all the time, not because they feel any doubt about their maleness but simply because it's something they associate with their sexual orientation. At the same time, there are people who have gone through life in this way thinking of themselves as gay who have, late in life, realised that they have probably been trans women all along. 'At the age of ninety, it has finally been explained to me that I am not really homosexual, I'm transgender. I now accept that,' noted the writer Quentin Crisp in a posthumously published autobiography. 'I went through life as though I was a boy in the outer world, but in my head I went on as though I were a woman. This explains why my life has been so strange.'[20]

A similar situation exists in the lesbian community, where there is an acknowledged overlap between butch identities and transmasculine identities. Although most butch lesbians identify firmly as female, this community has historically provided a safe place for trans men to adopt much of the social behaviour associated with men without facing the additional challenges of disassociating themselves entirely from the gender they are assumed to be. This has led to social tensions, with some lesbians accusing the nascent trans movement of 'stealing' lesbians, and this is also part of some older trans people's experience. The older he is, the more likely it is that a trans man who is attracted to women will have spent part of his life identifying as a lesbian, and the same is true of some transmasculine non-binary people. Where this experience has been positive, it's not uncommon for them to retain strong links to the lesbian community.

Expressions of sexual orientation can become still more complicated in situations where people have remained in relationships during transition. This can mean that the outside world perceives their partners' sexual orientation as having changed (if they were not bisexual to begin with), which can be quite unsettling for partners who feel that an important part of their identity hinges on being gay, lesbian or, indeed, heterosexual. This can be particularly challenging with late-life transitions because it's often harder to deal with having one's identity questioned after feeling secure in it for decades. This is one reason why it's important to consider counselling and social support for partners as well as for transitioning people themselves.

4

Transitioning in Later Life

The average age of transition used to be late 40s or early 50s – a time when, for a lot of people, their children had reached adulthood and they felt more at liberty to put themselves first. Now it is dropping all the time because it's much easier for young people to explore their gender and, where necessary, do something about it. But what about people who transition much later, towards the end of their lives?

Some people feel, at this point, that it's not worth it – that they've already missed the years that really mattered. Others assume that they wouldn't be accepted for treatment or that they couldn't get through the social change. Yet there are those who go ahead despite everything and say they couldn't be happier with the result.

For some people, feelings about gender change over the life course. They may be comfortable simply signalling their gender through clothing and language choices when young, but find as they get older that they are experiencing an increasing need for physiological change. It isn't necessary to have wanted hormones or surgery throughout your life in order for them to be the right choice for you. There is no evidence that people who decide to transition late in life are more likely to regret it.

Age can have an impact on every stage of transition – sometimes in negative ways but sometimes in positive ones. This chapter looks at what older people considering transition need to think about, and how others can help them.

Why come out?

Everybody has their own reasons for coming out as trans or non-binary. For most people, one of the key factors is simply wanting to feel comfortable in their own skin and find out what life is like without the constant pressure of trying to fit into a role that doesn't feel right. This can be worth doing even very late in life, with people who transition in their 80s and 90s reporting that it gives them a lot of joy just to be able to express themselves as they really are.

Some people cope with feelings of dysphoria throughout most of their lives simply by avoiding thinking about gender, but find that as they get older, they spend more time in single-sex spaces as a result of medical or care needs, which stops this coping mechanism from working as effectively. This can mean that it starts to feel necessary to talk to other people about an experience that has previously been kept private or shared only with loved ones.

Some people feel increasing pressure to come out as they get older because they don't want to die without anyone ever really knowing who they were. Even if they don't want to take on the challenge of changing how they live, they may want to be open with loved ones before it's too late.

Transition and family life

One of the greatest challenges for trans people who grew up in a society that didn't want to acknowledge their existence was finding ways to talk to family members about it. That's still difficult today, although more and more young people are now coming out before they have acquired dependants, meaning they have fewer tough conversations to face. For older generations, it has generally been easier to be open with partners and children than with parents, and it's not uncommon for people to wait for their parents to die before they feel able to express their gender.

The advantage of coming out as an older trans person is that any children you have are likely to be grown up with their own independent lives, so although you may still be concerned about how they'll react, it won't be as disruptive for them. You won't have to worry about them being bullied over it or about the challenges of looking after them if you have to manage getting to a lot of appointments during transition.

The end of a marriage is also a common reason for people to decide to come out in later life. It reduces the burden of responsibility to others and also, for many people, feels like a good opportunity for making a fresh start and focusing on personal needs. Friends are likely to be additionally supportive at such a time and more open to accepting dramatic changes.

If you rely on family members for help with care and day-to-day support – everything from getting you out and about in a wheelchair to helping with your shopping or coming in to do odd jobs in the house that you can no longer do for yourself – then you may be worried about the practical difficulties you could face if they react badly to you coming out, even if it's just an initial disagreement that can be overcome in time. Ask your doctor to put you in touch with social services so you can find out about the help that would be available to you in this situation. Local charities focused on age and disability may also be able to give you useful advice, or even help directly.

If you receive professional at-home care (including care provided by your local council) or if you live in a care home, you'll find a whole chapter of helpful information later in this book.

If you find that some family members are unhappy about your transition but they're still willing to try to understand, you may find that family counselling can help. This will involve you getting together with family members in a safe space where you can talk about your feelings, with a professional therapist steering the conversation and making sure that nobody bullies anybody else. It can help to clear up misunderstandings, address worries and remind your family members that you're still the same person.

Transition and friends

Sadly, it's not uncommon to lose friends when you come out as trans or non-binary. As we get older, we tend to have fewer friends, so this creates a risk of becoming socially isolated. On the other hand, long-standing friendships have usually weathered a few storms by this stage, and older people tend to be more willing to try to work through difficulties to hold on to what's good.

The biggest stumbling block that people report when they talk about how they came out late in life has to do with trust. Sometimes friends find it difficult to deal with the realisation that people they thought they were close to didn't trust them enough to come out sooner. They may feel that they have been actively lied to, or take it as a slight upon their character, feeling saddened that they could ever have been expected to react negatively. One way to decrease the risk of a response like this is to start by talking about the way that society has changed and discuss more general fears about fitting in, explaining that if one feels generally frightened about something, then it can be difficult to be rational. This helps to get across the point that your hesitation was nothing personal.

Coming to terms with the fact that a person one has known for years is not quite who they seemed to be can require a big adjustment. There can be confusion and strong emotions to begin with that quickly fade once there's been a bit of time to think about it all. If you're coming out to friends and asking them to make that adjustment for you, try to show them some patience in return. They may not have much understanding of the issues at all, they may have absorbed negative ideas that they'll soon shed once they recognise that those just don't make sense in light of what you're like as a friend, or they may simply feel a bit panicky and overwhelmed. Often people worry that they're going to say the wrong thing and cause offence, so they become more distant. If you suspect that this is happening, reassure them that you understand there's a lot to learn and you're not going to be angry or upset.

It's not all negative. In fact, many older trans people say that after they worried for years about the possible disasters that might stem from coming out, all of their friends told them they already knew. It's common for friends to suspect that there's something going on, even if they can't quite put their finger on it. Where older people are concerned, they often worry that secrets are being kept about a serious illness, so that when it emerges that the only issue is gender, their overwhelming feeling is one of relief.

Sometimes working through an experience like this can bring friends closer together and make the bond between them stronger. Some people feel excited to have been trusted with such a big thing, even if it did take a long time to reach that point. For others, it doesn't really feel like a big deal, or that feeling quickly recedes as they realise that being trans or non-binary is only part of who you are and that you're still basically the same person you always have been.

If you have always had a lot of friends of the same gender as you, you may find that they're happy and excited to discover that you're also a woman or also a man, because it makes them feel that you're an even better fit for their social circle. Some trans people experience a bit of love bombing as a result, being eagerly inducted into popular all-female or all-male activities. This can be overwhelming, so let people know if you prefer to take things slowly. You're going to need time to get used to a new way of living, and there's no need to rush into it, trying to do everything at once.

'I do have closer connections with women now than when younger,' says Sophie. 'Another positive aspect of social transition.'

Sometimes coming out as trans prompts other people to come out as gay, lesbian or bisexual, because they feel that being trans means you're more likely to be sympathetic or at least to take it in your stride. This can result in the relaxation of tensions that you didn't even know were there, and a closer, more rewarding friendship experience.

Transition and work

If you're still in work, you will once again find that there are pros and cons to coming out as an older trans or non-binary person. On the one hand, older workers are more vulnerable to being let go, and an unhappy boss may try to persuade you to take early retirement. On the other, if you've been working in the same place for a long time and everybody knows you well, you're likely to receive a lot more support than a less established worker. You may also be in a position where you know your job and the organisation you work for so well that you're considered indispensable.

The Equality Act 2010 protects trans people from discrimination in the workplace and means that your employer can't fire you because you come out. This means that if you suspect people in your workplace have figured out that you're trans and may not like it, coming out can actually put you in a stronger position. If you're in a union, it's a good idea to talk to your union rep first. You're within your rights to take them along to any meetings you may have with your boss or your HR manager to discuss issues relating to your gender.

Although prejudice and discrimination in the workplace remain a serious problem, many trans people do come out successfully at work and find that bosses and colleagues are supportive. Often work performance improves as a result.

Expressing your gender

What does it mean to come out socially as an older person? What will you want to change about your appearance and behaviour? Some people find that it's actually easier to gradually shift between gender roles as an older person because older people are seen as less sexual, and whether this is right or wrong in itself, it means that less attention is paid to their appearance by others. An unusual appearance is often chalked up to eccentricity and attracts less hostility than it might in someone younger.

In some ways, gender differences become less visible as we go through the later stages of the ageing process. Cis women's oestrogen levels drop significantly at menopause so their skin starts to look rougher (more like male skin) and they usually grow more body hair. Their Adam's apples may also become more prominent and their head hair is likely to get thinner. Meanwhile, because everybody loses muscle with age, older cis men tend to look smaller and narrower at the shoulders, losing some of their distinguishing bulk. This can make it easier to blend in.

Because of these changes, older people don't signal their gender in quite the same ways as younger people. For trans people who have little experience of presenting themselves in the way that feels right to them, it can be difficult to judge this correctly – you might have developed ideas of how you'd like to look based on images in the media, which are predominantly of younger people, and find that when you try them out, you don't really fit in with your peers. This can be a difficult thing to come to terms with because sometimes it compounds the sense of regret at years lost pretending to be something other than your true self. If you're keen to fit in, try to find role models your own age, but don't rule out presenting yourself in a more striking way sometimes for special occasions. There are times when it's nice to be noticed!

Changing your name

Changing your name is a relatively simple process which can be done through the post. It differs slightly in the different constituent nations of the UK.

In the UK, there is nothing illegal about using a name other than your given name. For most purposes, you can refer to yourself using whatever name you want. In order to change official documents such as your passport and driving licence, however, you will need some formal back-up. This will also help with changing your name on your financial records.

If you were born or adopted in England or Wales, the simplest way to change your name on official documents is by getting a deed poll. This can take the form of a simple declaration, using a template you can find online – you can do this straight away and many institutions will accept it as adequate proof that your name has changed. If you want to go a step further, you can apply to enrol your deed poll with the Royal Courts of Justice. This gives it more weight. Once you have an enrolled deed poll, every UK institution will be obliged to recognise your change of name.

If you were born or adopted in Scotland, you can change your name by statutory declaration. This can be drawn up and witnessed by a notary public or justice of the peace and recorded with the Registrar General. You can only change your first name once using this process (although you will still be free to use other names on an informal basis), so it's important to think carefully beforehand and be certain about your choice.

If you were born or adopted in Northern Ireland, you will need to fill out a change of name registration form and have it witnessed by a solicitor, lay magistrate or justice of the peace. You will then need to send it, along with your birth certificate, to the General Register Office for Northern Ireland, where it will be entered into the public record. As in Scotland, you can only change your first name once using this process.

It's important that you change your name on as many of your documents as you can immediately after getting a deed poll or registering a statutory declaration. This is actually a legal requirement if you have a driving licence, as you're required to keep it up to date. Getting your other documents changed reduces the risk that your new name will be challenged – that somebody will claim that it's not really the name you're using. Challenges like this are very rare and normally only occur where fraud is suspected, but it's a simple matter to protect yourself just in case.

Some trans people have a name they keep in mind throughout their lives that feels like their true name, making the choice of a new name easy. Some look at public records from around the time that they were born in order to find names that will seem very ordinary for people their age and help them go under the radar, whereas others take the opportunity to go for something that makes a statement. Some choose to use names similar to their given names, or preserve their original initials, because they feel this keeps things simple. Still others try to find out the names that their parents would have given them if their gender had been different at birth. If your parents are still alive, you may find that this is a very effective way to show your love for them and make them feel included in the transition process.

Changing your pronouns

For most people, one of the biggest steps in transition involves getting people to change the pronouns they use. For instance, you might want people to refer to you as *he* rather than *she*, but finding the right moment to make that change isn't always easy, especially if you want to come out to people a few at a time or if some people are reluctant to cooperate. After getting used to some people using a new pronoun for you, it can be more upsetting to hear other people using the wrong one. Some trans people use different pronouns in different contexts throughout their lives, however – what matters is that you take the time to work out what's likely to be best for you.

For older non-binary people, adopting a gender-neutral pronoun presents particular challenges. Awareness of such pronouns is quite a bit lower in older age groups, especially among people who don't use the internet, so you could find that the people you spend time with have difficulty getting used to it. There's a fair chance that they won't have met or even heard of anybody using such a pronoun before, so prepare yourself to do a lot of explaining.

You'll find a useful guide to popular non-binary pronouns in Appendix 2.

Older people who are aware of non-binary people often tend to assume that they're all young and are followers of a social fad or simply relate to society differently due to generational differences. It can be difficult for those who don't identify wholly or consistently with a male or female gender themselves to know where they fit in. If you're in this position, remember that you're not alone – there are many other people your age who have similar feelings, even if they're not very visible.

New pronouns can be particularly difficult to remember for people with dementia, even if it's still at a mild stage, because they often need to mentally refer back to older memories to retrieve information. They may find it easy to remember your gender because your appearance gives them a clue, yet find it harder to get the words right. Unless you want to start wearing a badge with your pronouns on it[21] (a popular choice for many young people in situations where they're meeting new people), there's no easy way to resolve this. You'll just have to take it in your stride and remember that mistakes don't usually indicate any intentional disrespect.

People often find it easier to remember that your pronouns have changed if it happens at the same time as another change – for instance, when you change your name, restyle your hair or start dressing full-time in clothes that express your true gender.

Psychological support and counselling

If you talk to your doctor about your gender, you can ask for a referral to a gender clinic. NHS waiting times are long in some parts of the country, but there are other forms of support available. More and more general counsellors and therapists are trained in gender diversity in both the public and private sectors, so if you're concerned that your feelings about your gender are impacting on other areas of your mental health (for instance, if you feel depressed or anxious), you can also ask your doctor to direct you to this type of support. The Pink Therapy Directory[22] provides a useful list of trans-friendly therapists around the UK.

Despite what you may have seen in the media, properly trained counsellors will not push you into changing the way you think about your gender. They're not there to tell you what you should think or what you should do, but to help you explore your own thoughts and feelings in a way that's helpful to you. It isn't necessary to reach any firm conclusions about your gender as you go through the counselling process, and if it's only a small part of what you want to talk about, that's fine too.

Although most people think of counselling as a one-to-one process, group counselling may also be an option for you. Some people say that they find group counselling with other LGBT people particularly helpful because it makes them feel more accepted. It can be a good way to work through internalised prejudice. Simply being trans doesn't mean being immune to the negative ideas about trans people that proliferate in our society, and sometimes we can be our own worst enemies. Seeing how other people are affected by this and similar issues can make it easier to process, so that you can start feeling more positive about yourself.

Some care homes and sheltered accommodation centres have developed relationships with counsellors who visit regularly and are open to talking about lots of different issues. They are unlikely to have trained in supporting trans or non-binary people (although there are professional resources they should be able to access in order to improve their understanding, if you ask them to), but they can help you with managing your feelings more generally. If you're living independently but struggle to get out of your house, ask your doctor if there is a district psychiatrist who can visit you to provide counselling support.

If it's difficult for you to get around and the above is not an option, or if there is nobody offering suitable counselling in your area, you may want to look at online options. Online counselling, usually provided through a platform such as Skype or Zoom so that you can still see the person you're talking to, is an increasingly popular option. While not everybody feels that it works for them without the reassurance of having somebody supportive in the same room, some find that it's very effective.

If neither in-person nor online counselling works for you, or if you want to explore issues around your mental health on your own before you start talking to other people about them, the NHS offers some good free tools through its website. These are designed to help you identify the type of problem you may have and work through your thoughts and feelings at a steady pace. The website also includes some thought exercises you can do to help you deal with problems like surges of panic or intrusive thoughts.

Sometimes coming to terms with being trans brings other issues to the surface. Things that you thought you were coping with, such as strained family relationships or childhood bullying, can become distressing again. If you initially sought out help because of issues around gender, don't feel that you're unable to talk about other issues too. The point of counselling is to help you feel more comfortable with who you are as a whole human being, and enable you to handle all the challenges you encounter in life more easily.

Hormonal transition

For most younger people who intend to undergo a binary transition (from male to female or from female to male), and for some non-binary people, hormones are the first and most urgent part of medically assisted transition. Hormones can have a significant direct effect in relieving dysphoria and also cause bodily changes that make you feel more comfortable in your skin. Taking oestrogen triggers breast growth and taking testosterone triggers the growth of facial hair. For older people, however, there are sometimes significant risks attached to such treatment. Your doctor will discuss this with you and, depending on your medical history and family history, you may end up deciding that it's best to use a low dose or not to use them at all.

For more information on the risks, see Chapter 6 on hormones and ageing later in this book.

If you are not able to have the same hormone treatment as most younger people, this doesn't mean that you won't be able to transition. Many people in this situation still opt to go through a social transition, and there may still be the option of surgery. Remember that there is no one true way to be trans or non-binary – you just need to work out the best way forwards for *you*.

Binding

Binding breasts to flatten the chest becomes more problematic with age for two reasons. First, the risk of developing tumours in the breast tissue increases, and compression of the breasts over prolonged periods is a known risk factor. Second, the risk of serious lung infections increases and the lungs generally begin to work less efficiently, so any further restriction on breathing becomes more dangerous. This does not mean, however, that binding must be completely ruled out. If you have specific concerns about it – for instance, if you have been finding it harder to breathe than usual or if you have a family history of breast cancer – discuss it with your doctor.

Some people find that their breasts lose mass as they get older so binding becomes less necessary. Wearing a sports bra or a suitable vest to stop the breasts moving around can sometimes be enough to reduce dysphoria.

If you wish to bind, use a binder that has been designed for the purpose, not bandages or tape. Restrict binding to short periods of time and don't do it every day. Consider options like disguising your shape with big chunky jumpers or heavy shirts the rest of the time. For most people, it remains safe to bind occasionally – so that you can look good in a suit for a special event, for instance.

Breast removal and chest reconstruction

Surgical procedures to remove unwanted breast tissue can still be carried out in most older people even if other surgery is ruled out, because it's usually possible to carry out the work under a local anaesthetic (with or without accompanying sedation). This is easier when the breasts are smaller to begin with, and smaller breasts also mean that it can usually be done more quickly, reducing the overall quantity of anaesthetic that needs to be used. As most people with breasts lose fatty tissue from them during their later years, this is something that can actually get easier with time.

Although reducing the size of breasts is relatively simple, reconstructing the chest to give it a more masculine appearance presents a different set of challenges. At present there is only one place in the UK where this kind of work is done on the NHS (which is, to the delight of pun-lovers, in Manchester), so the need to travel can be a barrier for older people. Reconstruction requires a longer period of anaesthetic use and can take a greater toll on the body, so you're unlikely to be offered this procedure unless your doctor feels that you have a good level of overall physical fitness.

Most trans men find that breast reduction is enough to help them look good with their clothes on, and that it can relieve dysphoria quite a bit. Building up the biceps – which becomes much easier if you're taking testosterone – distracts the eye and makes people notice breasts less. Trans men usually need chest reconstruction, however, if they want to feel fully confident about the way they look when topless.

Breast enhancement

Breasts develop naturally in the presence of a certain level of oestrogen in the blood, so as soon as trans women start taking hormones they begin to change shape. In trans women, however, breasts tend to be slightly smaller than in cis women, and because most trans women also have wider than average shoulders, they may not look proportionate. Many trans women in this situation – along with those who are unable to or don't want to take hormones – opt for breast enhancement surgery in order to give themselves a more natural or satisfying shape.

For older women, the situation is slightly more complex. Older cis women's breasts tend to lose some mass and sag a little, so newly constructed or enhanced breasts can look unnaturally perky – not necessarily a problem, but something that can make it harder to blend in. Of course, there are also cis women who choose to undergo these procedures in later life, so this is becoming less of a problem – it's really an issue of thinking through how much you want to draw attention to yourself. Some surgeons can adapt their technique to create a more natural appearance that fits with your age.

If you want to experiment to find out what sort of shape you would be most comfortable with before you go for surgery, you can buy breast forms online and simply slot them into your bra. Most surgeons now also offer computer modelling, which helps to give you an impression of how your new breasts will look before you have them constructed.

Genital surgery for trans women

There are several different types of genital surgery available for trans women (and sometimes also chosen by non-binary people). Even if your doctor says that some are unsuitable for you, others may remain a possibility.

The simplest and most common surgery of this type is orchiectomy – the removal of the testicles. This has two benefits. First, it removes one of the more noticeable physical characteristics associated with maleness, thus helping to reduce dysphoria for some people and making it easier to dress discreetly. Second, it removes the main natural source of testosterone production in the body, something which often drastically reduces dysphoria and, over time, reduces the appearance of some masculine secondary sexual characteristics. Losing testosterone like this also has negative effects, however, such as increasing your risk of bone problems as you get older, unless you are able to take oestrogen, which does some of the same jobs. An endocrinologist can help you to work out the healthiest option for your body.

Vaginal construction is a lengthy surgical procedure and follow-up surgeries are sometimes needed, so you will need to be in good health to be able to go through this. To get good results, a lot of follow-up care is required. You will normally need to be able to get in and out of a bath and use a dilator several times a week to keep your new vagina healthy as it heals. Although some people find that this is no longer necessary after a few months or years, others need to do it on an ongoing basis to prevent shrinkage from occurring (something that can also be a problem for cis women), so you'll need to think about how you will manage this if it becomes harder for you to do things for yourself.

Vaginal construction doesn't automatically involve the construction of a clitoris (historically, some male doctors have argued that a clitoris is not very important), so if this matters to you, it's another thing you'll have to discuss. It will mean being under anaesthetic for longer, which always entails more risk, but it is not in itself a particularly risky procedure and surgeons are getting increasingly good results. Some women – trans and cis – feel that the clitoris gets more important to them as they get older because it provides a means of achieving sexual satisfaction that doesn't require penetration, and therefore one that can work even with the lower energy levels and aches and pains that age can bring.

A surgically constructed vagina will not naturally lubricate, so if you want it to be able to be penetrated during sexual activity, you will need to use lubricating gel. If you're using a latex condom, this gel will need to be water-based, not oil-based, so that it doesn't damage the condom. Some trans women worry that using lube forces them to come out as trans or makes them seem less naturally feminine, but this is less of an issue when you're older, as a significant number of post-menopausal cis women need to use it too.

It is possible to have your penis removed without going through vaginal construction. This is a much simpler operation and you won't need to be under anaesthetic for as long, which makes it safer. Your surgeon can simply construct a small hole for you to urinate through. If you choose this, however, it will be difficult for you to change your mind later and decide that you do want a vagina, because skin from the penis is normally used in the construction process. There are some alternative options but the results are unlikely to be as good.

What constitutes the best option for you will also depend to an extent on your sex life. If you regularly play a receiving role in penetrative sex, this may actually help a new vagina to stay healthy, although you should be prepared for it to be uncomfortable at first. If you are currently sexually inactive and have reached an age where you don't expect to have another sexual relationship, having a vagina may not matter very much to you. Some trans women still feel a strong need for one in order to feel complete, but for others it's enough to feel generally feminine in shape and be perceived as female by other people.

Genital surgery for trans men

Genital reconstruction for trans men is more complex. There are two different ways of building a phallus. Phalloplasty produces the larger organ of the two, but one that cannot become erect on its own; it is possible to create an erection discreetly using a pump. Metoidioplasty builds on the clitoris to create an organ that can become erect on its own but is significantly smaller, and it is difficult to carry out this form of surgery on somebody who has not had hormone treatment.

It's also possible to implant artificial testicles, a simple procedure which usually remains safe even very late in life, although it involves stretching the skin and can therefore be more uncomfortable when this has lost its youthful elasticity. Additionally, there is the option of closing up the vagina, which is a difficult procedure with a significant degree of risk attached, to the point where many young and healthy trans men opt not to undergo it.

For some trans men, genital reconstruction is very important and getting it done greatly relieves dysphoria. For others, top surgery is sufficient because it enables them to blend in among other men in day-to-day life. Urinating in public toilets can be managed discreetly by using a prosthetic or simply going into a stall, which many older cis men do anyway simply because they find it easier. Many trans men who don't have bottom surgery still have active sex lives with partners who respect their gender.

If you think that genital surgery could be helpful to you, ask your doctor for advice. They will be able to assess your personal level of risk and help you to work out the best way forward.

Older trans role models

One of the challenges of transitioning in later life is that it can be hard to find role models you can relate to. Most trans people you're likely to see on television or in the newspapers are in their 20s and 30s, with very different life experiences. They don't face the same physical issues and most of them have grown up with better social support, or at least with the awareness that there are other people like them. Faced with this, it can be difficult to find people to relate to – people whose stories can help you to make sense of your own.

There are still very few older trans people in the public eye. Historically, coming out as trans has been considered a good way to end a career, and has either been hushed up or so loudly derided by the media that it has discouraged such individuals from remaining in the spotlight. Notable exceptions include model April Ashley and tennis player Renée Richards, both of whom managed to carve out their own social spaces despite coming out. Other older trans people have made a name for themselves in niche areas – for instance, as scientists or business people – but without being visible to most members of the public. Examples of prominent older trans men and non-binary people are particularly thin on the ground.

This shortage of visible older trans people has an effect not just on trans people themselves but also on their cis peers, who may see being trans as a fad among younger people and find it harder to understand as a result. One recent study[23] found that Caitlyn Jenner coming out seems to have reduced transphobia among older Americans who followed her story in the media, and that this in turn made those people less likely to oppose policies aimed at improving trans people's legal position.

5

Age and Bodily Change

All bodies change with age, altering the way we look, the way we move and the way we present ourselves to others. This can also affect the way that we express gender and the way other people interpret it. This brings mixed blessings for trans and non-binary people. Although age can make it harder to maintain some characteristics – such as smooth skin and well-defined muscle – that are important in conveying identity, some people feel that it's easier to blend in as an older person and that older people in general face less pressure to conform to particular standards of appearance.

'I'm more confident now to express my gender as I care less and less what other people's judgement may be. I wonder if young people tend to see old people as less gendered but it still feels very important to me,' said Rowan.

Trans people have the same concerns and anxieties about getting older as anyone else. Sometimes what feels good because it eases feelings of dysphoria can also feel bad because it's not very flattering, leading to confusion and even a sense of guilt. There are also medical issues to consider and it's important to make sure that you get all the health checks you need, even if some of them feel uncomfortably at odds with your gender. You will need to be prepared to be proactive about this as some doctors don't have a good understanding of trans issues, but you'll find that the majority of healthcare professionals are supportive and helpful.

Cancer risks

As you get older, your risk of developing certain cancers increases. The NHS offers screening to increase the chance that if you do develop cancer, it will be caught early, when it's still comparatively easy to treat. It's important to make sure that you attend the right screenings. The NHS is getting increasingly good at recognising trans people's needs and sending out the right screening invitations, but if you have any doubts, you should talk to your doctor or to a nurse at your regular well man or well woman clinic (if you are non-binary, go to the one you feel most comfortable with).

Trans men remain at risk of developing cervical cancer if they still have cervical tissue, and remain at risk of developing breast cancer if they still have breast tissue, regardless of hormone use or other surgery.

The evidence remains unclear on trans women's risk of developing prostate cancer, but as it's clear that at least some risk remains, they are advised to follow the same screening programmes as men. The NHS also advises trans women to get screened for breast cancer, even though their risk appears to be significantly lower than that faced by cis women.

If you are uncomfortable about going to a clinic for a screening because you're worried about being outed or you think you might be harassed, phone ahead and ask for advice. The staff will do all they can to ensure that you can get the care you need discreetly. Some screenings can be carried out at your GP's surgery. If at any point you feel discriminated against because you're trans, you can point out that this breaches the Equality Act 2010.

Skincare

For transfeminine people who have enjoyed seeing hormone treatment soften their skin, it can be dispiriting to deal with it getting rougher again due to the effects of ageing. Two things help to compensate for this: first, because their cis female peers are experiencing a similar change, it doesn't make them look unusual; second, if they are continuing to take hormones, then their skin will continue to look better than that of cis women not on HRT, who will actually have lower levels of oestrogen in their bodies post-menopause.

Why, if oestrogen remains stable, do skin changes happen at all? The answer is that although oestrogen helps skin in some ways, there's only so much it can do. Chemically, it plays two key roles: it helps to trap moisture in the skin, making it plump and soft; and it increases production of collagen, the tissue that gives skin its elasticity and keeps it from cracking. Both of these factors help to prevent lines from forming in the skin, which is part of the reason why wrinkling increases with age. (Because cis men also produce some natural oestrogen which declines with age, they also experience this effect.)

Other factors that we associate with age, however, have nothing to do with oestrogen. Most notably, a natural process that flattens skin cells as they move outwards in the epidermis slows down. This means that instead of being like a layer of closely fitted tiles, the skin surface becomes a collection of tiny spheres, giving it a rougher texture and making pores look bigger. The only way to smooth skin like this effectively is to use a face cream or foundation that fills in all those tiny dents (and smaller lines) without suffocating the skin. There's no need to pay through the nose for this – there are a lot of low-cost products on the market that do a good job.

Fat redistribution

Trans and non-binary people who take oestrogen or testosterone will be familiar with the way that these hormones cause fat to be redistributed on the face and body, often giving a more satisfying gendered appearance. This process usually begins quite quickly but it takes a few years to reach optimum – another reason why trans people often feel better about their looks as they get older even when their cis peers are starting to feel more self-conscious.

In later life, however, other factors begin to affect fat distribution, and the facial profile, in particular, tends to become leaner and more masculine, even for transfeminine people who continue to take oestrogen. The effects of this are usually not very pronounced but they can lead to insecurity in transfeminine people, whereas transmasculine people may find them advantageous. For those who struggle with these changes, there are make-up techniques that can help by drawing attention to the more feminine aspects of the face. YouTube is full of free tutorial videos explaining these. Simple plastic surgery procedures are also an option. Done professionally, they're low risk and can be carried out on an outpatient basis, but they may need to be repeated as frequently as every six months.

Bone structure

For transmasculine people using testosterone, there's one particular benefit to getting older, and that's a gradual change in bone structure. Prolonged use of testosterone slowly causes the bones on the face to broaden, so that the jaw looks stronger and the zygomatic arch is enhanced. Meanwhile, some broadening of the shoulders may also occur. These changes are effectively turned off in trans women who have had their testicles removed or use anti-androgens.

Non-binary people with testicles who have not taken hormones because they're comfortable with their bodies should be aware of these changes, which are most dramatic in later life but can start in the early 30s, so that they can consider how they feel about them before it's too late to take preventative action. Once they have occurred, there's no way to undo some of them and others can only be undone using expensive, specialist cosmetic surgery.

Muscle loss

The loss of muscle fibres, or sarcopenia, is a normal part of the ageing process. From around the age of 30, most people lose 3–5 per cent of their muscle mass per year, with the average cis man losing 30 per cent of his muscle mass over his lifetime. This can be particularly distressing for transmasculine people who rely on muscle definition as a key means of communicating their gender to others. It's important to note, however, that there is a difference between the loss of muscle fibres and the loss of a muscular appearance.

Muscle fibres are, in effect, the levers that allow muscles to move. If you have more of them, you'll find it easier to build strength, but if you never exercise them, you'll still be weak compared with somebody with slightly fewer muscle fibres who keeps them in good condition. This is because the individual fibres themselves need to be built up and maintained in order to be effective. When we talk about building muscle, we're not talking about creating more muscle fibres – something that's very difficult to do in humans – but about strengthening the ones we've got. This means that regular working out – without overdoing it – can still keep you in good shape. You'll just have to work a little harder as you get older.

If you're regularly taking testosterone, you should be wary about using muscle-building supplements, some of which are designed to increase natural testosterone production and can do so to some extent whether or not you have testicles. You don't necessarily absorb the extra testosterone but could end up with more of it in your blood. This is associated with a higher risk of illnesses such as strokes and heart attacks which are already more common in the later years of life. If you really want to try a supplement to help keep your body in shape, discuss it with your doctor first. The best option may simply be a diet rich in vegetable-derived proteins.

If you suffer from a high degree of muscle loss and become frail as you age, remember that a lot of cis men go through this too and there are other ways to express masculinity. It's difficult to adjust to, but most men find that the psychological impact decreases with time.

Hair loss

Almost everybody experiences some hair loss as they age. For transmasculine people, an increased risk of going wholly or partially bald is one of the side effects of testosterone use. The good news for transfeminine people taking oestrogen is that it usually brings the development of male pattern baldness to an abrupt end, and some trans women insist that they have actually experienced hair regrowth, although there is no scientific data to back this up.

It's important that trans people taking oestrogen and transmasculine people who have not had their ovaries removed do not use hair-loss treatments designed for men as these can actually be dangerous in the presence of significant amounts of oestrogen in the body. Transmasculine people who have had their ovaries removed should discuss the matter with a doctor before trying a treatment like this.

Hair renewal products in which minoxidil is the active ingredient are generally considered safe for any adult to use. There are also other tricks you can use if you still have hair but worry that it looks too thin. Basic moisturising shampoos and conditioners will help hair retain more moisture, making it look fuller and healthier. There are slightly more sophisticated products available that insert protein structures and nutritious oils into individual hair strands to make them thicker, an approach that also improves hair elasticity and makes it more resistant to breaking. Don't be put off by the cost of some of these products – there are low-cost versions which are just as effective. You can also find a good range of products that are not tested on animals or are suitable for vegans, so everyone should be able to find something they feel comfortable with.

Thinning hair can look more obvious if it contrasts strongly with the colour of the scalp, so simply dyeing your hair can help to disguise the problem. Avoid using dyes containing bleach, which leave hair more brittle, and avoid styles that strain the hair, such as tight buns, braids or cornrows.

Hair gain

While head hair tends to recede with age, body hair and facial hair usually increases and even sprouts in new places. This can be unsettling for transfeminine people. On the positive side, because cis women are going through this too, hair that they may always have struggled to get rid of entirely stops being so closely associated with gender.

Most hair removal techniques remain viable in later life. Some people will find that the surface of their skin is more easily damaged, so they will need to give up on abrasive techniques and aggressive depilatory creams. It's usually necessary to use a strong moisturising ointment after electrolysis at this age even if it wasn't in the past. For people who struggle to get out and about, home laser hair removal kits are now widely available. They don't work well on very fine hair but are usually very effective otherwise.

For many trans men and transmasculine people, increased facial hair comes as a blessing. Most people instantly identify someone with a thick, natural beard or moustache as male, regardless of other characteristics, and visible body hair can have a similar effect. You will need to learn how to groom it properly, but many barbers are happy to give advice on this and you can also find helpful instructional videos online.

Vocal changes

As we get older, our bodies have more difficulty in retaining moisture pretty much everywhere, and one thing that affects is the voice. This is because dry vocal cords don't vibrate as much, leading the voice to sound thin and wavery. Trans men may find that they lose some of the depth in their voices that they worked hard to gain, though this doesn't necessarily mean that people will think they sound female, as their cis peers' voices will be changing in the same way and they will still, in most cases, have picked up male patterns of speech which also make a difference to how people interpret gender.

Trans women are often encouraged to speak softly as a means of conveying femininity even if they can't raise the pitch of their voices as much as they'd like to. Unfortunately, this can become more difficult with age as stiffening of the vocal cords can permanently distort their shape, making the voice sound rougher. This is a much bigger risk if you smoke. You can decrease the risk by gently exercising your voice every day. Singing scales is a good way to go about this as long as you're careful to avoid doing too much and causing strain. The ideal place to do it is the bathroom because warm, moist air reduces the risk of damage.

Overall, cis women's voices tend to get lower with age while cis men's get slightly higher. The effect of this is that trans people start to sound more like their peers. If you find that you start to have less control of your voice, try to rest it completely at intervals through the day and especially in the run-up to social activity. Your vocal cords, like other muscles, can get tired and are better at doing their job as desired when they've had the chance to relax. It also helps to stay well hydrated.

Developing a personal style

Many of the people who contributed their opinions to this book felt that it had become easier for them, over time, to develop a personal sense of style that suited who they were – an experience shared with the cis population. For trans people, there is often an awkward period directly following social transition that's similar to what cis people go through in adolescence, when some experimenting needs to be done to work out what looks good and sends the right messages to others. As the years go by, it becomes easier to make choices about clothes and other aspects of personal presentation, so that confidence in one's appearance tends to increase.

'My appearance has evolved as my style has changed,' said Stephanie. 'I have a distinct fashion sense and I frequently end up shopping online for interesting clothing. Having said that, as an artist I have to be somewhat pragmatic about what I wear as I am frequently going into dirt-filled environments. I have become a lot more comfortable in who I am.'

Although some trans people struggle because of the shortage of role models to help them make their way through life, others find this liberating, especially when it comes to getting older. They feel that they are under less pressure than their cis counterparts to present themselves in ways that are seen as age-appropriate, and they enjoy the freedom to experiment. Some also have a more sanguine attitude to matters like putting on weight or developing wrinkles than cis people tend to, because they have overcome such big hurdles to feel comfortable with the way they look that these things seem trivial. This gives them enhanced confidence, which other people tend to find attractive and socially appealing.

6

Hormone Use and Ageing

Many (though not all) binary trans people, and some non-binary people, take hormones in order to change the way they feel and the way that their bodies express secondary sexual characteristics. Although a few people have health conditions that complicate or preclude this, for most younger people it's fairly straightforward. From the age of 50, however, it can become more complicated. Cis people's bodies go through a natural process of hormonal realignment at around this age (it's more noticeable in women – as menopause – but happens in men too), and trans and non-binary people may need to adjust their hormone medication in order to stay healthy.

Two principal factors influence how hormone medication affects the bodies of trans and non-binary people. The first is how old they are. The second is how long they have been taking it. There is still a limited amount of research in this area because only a small number of people who started taking cross-sex hormones early in life have reached old age, but most doctors believe that the risk of complications is likely to be different for late transitioners compared with those who have taken hormones for a long time.

This chapter explores some of the risks associated with hormone treatment in later life and looks at ways they can be managed.

If you have any worries as a result of reading this chapter, discuss them with your doctor. Never abruptly stop taking your hormones without medical supervision as this could cause serious health problems in itself.

Hormone treatment and cis people

Despite the shortage of trans people who can be studied in order to understand more about hormone use and ageing, there is some useful data from the cis population that gives us an idea of what to expect. This comes mostly from women taking HRT, women taking additional oestrogen after having their ovaries removed for health reasons, men taking testosterone after having their testicles removed for health reasons, and people receiving additional hormones after undergoing aggressive chemotherapy or radiotherapy which has interfered with their natural hormone production.

There is also a small amount of data from people who have been given oestrogen or testosterone as a treatment for intersex variations, but this is limited due to a stigma about intersex which historically (and still today in some countries) resulted in a lot of medical records being destroyed.

Drawing on this data has helped experts to build up a profile of the risks associated with taking oestrogen or testosterone and how they change over time. These risks are more significant if you have a family history of any of the medical problems in question. If this is the case, you should let your doctor know about it when considering the best way to go forward with your treatment.

Healthy hormone levels

As you get older, it's more important than ever to make sure that you have adequate hormone levels to maintain your general health. Your bones will become more fragile and your balance will gradually become poorer so falling is both more likely and more dangerous, but oestrogen and testosterone can both play a role in protecting your bones, as can getting plenty of low-impact exercise (such as walking).

Maintaining the right hormone levels in later life is a balancing act, with different health concerns emerging if they're too low or too high. The good news for trans people is that problems are more likely to be spotted early due to ongoing monitoring, and artificially administered hormones are much easier to adjust than internally produced ones. It's important to keep getting blood tests done even if declining general health makes getting to the doctor difficult. For people who have real difficulty getting out and about, district nurses are usually happy to visit to take blood samples.

'I don't really feel that I have an alternative but to keep taking hormones,' said Kirsty. 'The risks are there, but to stop or even significantly reduce the dosage is unthinkable. My GP is supportive but he just doesn't have the specialist knowledge and it is to his credit that he would admit this rather than try to bluff. Endo[crinology] are generally uncommunicative – I go there for blood tests every six months and then hear nothing. They say I'll only hear from them if there's a problem with my results.'

Weight gain

Most healthy people find that they gain a bit of weight as they get older. For trans women, the first few years of hormone treatment can trigger a significant weight increase and also tend to make the weight more visible because of the way it's redistributed around the body. On the plus side, this creates a more feminine shape, but in combination with ageing it increases the risk of developing a number of health problems. The right diet and exercise programme can help with staying in shape, so this should be discussed with a doctor or your local well woman clinic.

'I don't mind the physical risks (although weight gain is a pain!), as the psychological advantages far outweigh those risks,' said Sophie.

For trans men, the situation is slightly different. Many trans men strive to be thin pre-transition in order to keep their breasts from becoming more prominent, and this can set lifelong habits. Others work out at various points in their lives with the aim of developing a more muscular physique. Testosterone does lead to increased appetite, however, and if physical activity declines with age, then unhealthy weight gain can become a risk later in life. This is additionally problematic because trans men already face an elevated risk of cardiac disorders. Trans men who feel that they are starting to gain weight in an unhealthy way should check with their doctor both for advice on diet and exercise and to make sure that the dose of testosterone they are taking remains safe for them.

Temperature sensitivity

Many people taking oestrogen report that it makes them much more sensitive to changes in temperature. This occurs because oestrogen causes vasodilation (relaxing of the blood vessels) and it can become more acute with age. There's no simple solution, but you should be aware that if you are a trans woman or a transfeminine non-binary person on hormones and you seem to feel the cold more than your cis peers and more than the men around you, it's likely to be a real experience, not just something you're imagining. Wrap up warm and don't feel awkward about turning to hot water bottles or heat packs for comfort – many younger people use them too. At the other end of the scale, you may find that you need to start drinking your coffee or tea at a cooler temperature to avoid discomfort.

Blood pressure

Getting older increases the risk of health problems caused by blood pressure that is too high or too low. Whether you are trans, non-binary or cis, this is strongly affected by the hormones in your body.

Trans men, like cis men, are particularly at risk of developing high blood pressure. There are several very effective treatments for this, so it may not mean that testosterone needs to be reduced, although some trans men find that to be the easiest solution. If you are diagnosed with high blood pressure, then you may have to take daily medication for the rest of your life, but you can reduce the risk of getting into this situation – and the risk of the serious health problems associated with it – through regular aerobic exercise and a healthy diet.

The vasodilation caused by oestrogen means that trans women are at a lower risk of developing high blood pressure, but sometimes this effect can mask other problems, so it's a good idea to monitor your blood pressure regularly (usually every one to three days, in accordance with your doctor's advice) if you have to stop or reduce your oestrogen either temporarily or permanently. You can buy a blood pressure monitor to use at home if you want to – it's easy to do – or you can get help from your GP's surgery or visit one of the many pharmacies that offer this service for free.

Older trans women face an increased risk of developing low blood pressure. This can be chronic, in which case daily medication may be needed, or it can be what's called orthostatic low blood pressure, which causes sudden feelings of faintness or dizziness when standing up from a seated position or sitting up from a lying position. Sometimes orthostatic low blood pressure can be exacerbated by short-term illnesses or dehydration. It's dangerous in older people because it increases the risk of falling, but most people learn to cope with it simply by moving more slowly and making sure they have something to hold on to as they rise.

Unrelated illness

As you get older, your risk of developing serious illness increases and you become more likely to need to take other medication on a long-term basis or go into hospital for more intensive treatments. This can complicate your hormone regime. Always try to discuss the fact that you're taking hormones at an early stage after diagnosis. In some cases, it can actually give you an advantage, reducing some of the risks associated with treatment. In other cases, it will affect what your doctors decide is the best type of treatment for you.

Some doctors who are not used to looking after trans patients become fixated on hormones in a way that distracts from their ability to provide proper care. This is known colloquially as *trans broken arm syndrome* – a tendency to try to link everything to transness even when there's an obvious unrelated cause, such as just having been hit by a car. If this happens, don't be shy about calling the doctor out on it. Remember that you are always entitled to a second opinion.

Surgery

Getting older also means that you're more likely to need surgery and that the risks of going under general anaesthetic increase. If you are scheduled to have an operation, talk to your doctor about your hormones. You may be asked to stop taking them for a few weeks beforehand. Although this may make you feel odd and uncomfortable, it will not normally be for long enough for you to have to worry about unwanted gender characteristics returning.

It's important to do as your doctor advises because this will make your operation much safer.

In order to work around these issues, you may find that you are offered the option of having a local anaesthetic, with or without sedation, for some operations where a general anaesthetic is normally used. If this sounds frightening, remember that caesarean sections are routinely performed this way without problems. As long as you communicate well with medical staff, you will be all right. If you have sedation, the chances are that you will barely remember the experience.

Unanswered questions

The fact that trans people taking hormones are now growing older has the potential to answer some long-standing medical questions, with the potential to help cis people as well. For instance, it could help us to determine whether the fact that, on average, men die younger than women is caused by testosterone or some other factor associated with maleness. It is already helping to clarify the role of hormones in some types of cancer.

Trans people going through medical treatment are increasingly being invited to participate in studies to help with this building of knowledge. If this happens to you, remember that you always have the right to say no – even after the study has begun – if you feel uncomfortable about it. Usually, though, it just involves answering a few questions on matters you would be discussing with your doctor anyway, and your confidentiality will be protected.

7

Retirement Planning

Studies show that trans people are significantly more likely than most to have difficulty finding work[24] and experience periods of unemployment.[25] This means that many approach retirement with little in the way of private pension funds or savings, so good planning and money management become much more important. You will need to know how to look after the funds that you do have, identify the support that's available and make sure that you are able to remain in control of your resources.

Managing money

When approaching retirement, most people can benefit from undertaking a thorough review of their finances. The aim of this is to identify and cut off any unnecessary outgoings (often little things like subscriptions which accumulate over the years and get forgotten about), and to identify any overlooked sources of income. It can also help you to make sure that any savings you have are earning a good rate of interest and that you're not paying more tax than you need to. It gives you the chance to consolidate any debts you have so that you're paying less in interest, and to work out how you can get the most out of any existing investments.

There are two ways of going about this. If you have a substantial amount of assets, it's almost always worthwhile hiring a professional accountant, who will often be able to save you more money than you pay in fees. If you don't have very much or if you're confident that you can manage it yourself, it is possible to take a DIY approach, but you will need to be very thorough. Be prepared to do a lot of digging through old documents. Start with your bank statements (including those for savings accounts) and work through them to track every detail of your incoming and outgoing funds. Investigate anything that strikes you as unusual – even if it only concerns a small amount and if you have to go to a great deal of trouble to get to the bottom of it.

If you need to track payments further back and you don't have all your bank statements around, your bank will usually be happy to print new ones for you from its records. Some banks actually offer to help their older customers with undertaking a financial review, and even if they don't, they are often happy to provide free financial advice.

State pensions

State pensions are based on an individual's recorded sex. In most cases, this means sex as designated at birth. Where trans people are concerned, birth-designated sex applies unless there is a gender recognition certificate. This means that, prior to 2018, the presence or absence of a gender recognition certificate affected when a person was deemed to have reached pensionable age. This means that older trans women without gender recognition certificates have often remained in work for longer than is typical of their cis peers, or are less financially secure.

If you are still working when you transition and you get a gender recognition certificate, it will be automatically sent to the central office of the Department for Work and Pensions (DWP) so that your details can be updated. It's often easiest if you change your name at the same time, as you are only entitled to one new National Insurance card in the course of your life (something that can create a problem for detransitioners). A restricted notice will be put on your account so that none of your previous details are visible to ordinary staff.

If you don't have a gender recognition certificate, you won't be able to change your gender in official records, but if you send in a letter from your doctor confirming that you're trans, any future communications will be addressed to you using the appropriate pronouns and title. Unfortunately, there is no system in place to recognise non-binary people.

Private pensions

Because, prior to 2014, it was necessary to divorce in order to get a gender recognition certificate (or, if in a civil partnership, to have it dissolved) – and because this remains a necessity in Northern Ireland, and also in England and Wales in the event of a spouse refusing to cooperate – trans people often find that they lose out on some of the survivor benefits they would otherwise have been entitled to. This can also be a problem for their spouses or former spouses if they die first. Where they have remarried or entered into a civil partnership with the same person after being legally single for long enough to obtain the certificate, this is treated as a new marriage and survivor benefits related to the earlier marriage are not carried over.

In light of this, it's important to check your standing with any private pensions you have if you are or have been married to a trans person, or if you are a trans person wanting to plan for your spouse or civil partner as well as yourself. You may not be able to recover lost money, but at least you'll be able to plan from an informed perspective and won't suddenly discover that funds you thought you could depend on are not there.

Equity release

If you're a homeowner and you feel that you're reaching the last years of your life, it can be tempting to sign up to an equity release agreement and start using the money in your home to do nice things for yourself. This is a particular temptation for late transitioners who may feel that they missed out on opportunities early in life. Some people use it to pay for private treatments, such as facial feminisation or masculinisation treatment, which they would not otherwise be able to afford.

It's important to recognise that freeing up equity in property is like paying off a mortgage in reverse. You will gradually own less and less of your home, and even if your agreement says that you can continue to live in it until the end of your days, you won't be able to sell it and the estate you leave to loved ones after you die could end up being worth substantially less.

State benefits

Getting older entitles you to a range of state benefits not available to the wider population, and means that some others on which you may have been depending cease to be available. You may be eligible for Attendance Allowance if you need care but you will not qualify for Personal Independence Payment after you reach the age of 65. You may be able to get a reduction in your Council Tax, you may qualify for Housing Benefit, and for those living in England where prescription charges apply, you won't have to pay for prescriptions after you turn 60. In many areas, free access to public transport is available to help you get around.

State benefits agencies have a good reputation for protecting sensitive personal data where trans people are concerned. They will always refer to you by the title you request even if you don't have a gender recognition certificate.

If you are unsure about how to access the benefits you may be entitled to, you will find useful information on the government's website. Citizens Advice can help you, and many charities focused on older people can also provide assistance, up to and including a full review of your financial circumstances.

Discounts and special arrangements

As well as getting help from the state, you'll find that getting older means you have access to a range of discounts from public and privately run institutions, many of which will also be happy to make special arrangements for you to ensure that you still have access. For many trans and non-binary people who have struggled earlier in life, this means suddenly having access to a new set of cultural opportunities that could enable you to meet new people and make new friends with interests similar to your own.

Prioritising

Support services committed to helping people who encounter financial difficulties as they get older often face a communication gap with trans people because they don't understand their priorities. This can range from struggling to appreciate why money saved for cosmetic surgery is about managing dysphoria rather than indulging a trivial desire, to not understanding why a trans person needing to move into cheaper or more accessible accommodation has to rule out certain areas for safety reasons.

If you're finding it hard to access the help you're entitled to because of something like this, there are two main options open to you. One is to ask if the service provider has an equalities officer you can speak to, who can help to explain the issues you're facing. The other is to bring in an advocate to stand up for you. This can be somebody you know socially or it can be someone from a professional advocacy organisation who has the right background to understand your circumstances and appreciate the additional challenges you face.

Although it's understandable that some support providers may struggle the first time they encounter a situation like yours, they have a legal obligation to ensure that they don't discriminate against you for being trans. This doesn't just mean that they should be polite and respect your gender – it also means that they should make an effort to understand your needs, and not just write you off as difficult because you're trans.

Financial abuse

Because we all tend to need more practical help from others as we get older, and because there is an expectation that older people will have difficulty understanding modern finance tools and systems or will be more confused generally, getting older goes along with an increased risk of falling victim to financial abuse. This takes two main forms: abuse by strangers running scams, and abuse by relatives trying to take control of savings or personal funds.

The most common scams involve unsolicited phone calls or email, so exercising caution about these things can do a lot to keep you safe. Never give out information directly to somebody who contacts you in this way. If you're told that there's a problem with your bank account, your pension or something similar, contact the organisation concerned directly by the usual means – don't use any new links or numbers that you've been given. Any genuine financial organisation will respect your caution and not pressure you.

Although there is no indication that trans people are at increased risk from financial scams in general, there's some evidence that those who have yet to transition or have done so only recently are less likely to have the confidence to assert themselves in high-pressure situations. Remember that you are always within your rights to put the phone down, block people online or even shut your door in someone's face if you're worried that they may not be genuine. Again, those who are genuine will understand and will think no less of you.

Because many trans people have strained relationships with their families, the risk of falling victim to financial abuse by relatives is higher. It can be hard to say no when somebody you love but haven't had much contact with asks for a loan – even if it's the third time and you've never been paid back. Other forms of abuse are more subtle, such as relatives persuading you that you're starting to get worse at decision making – or simply find it tiring – so you'll be safer if they look after your money for you, then slowly bleeding it away. Sometimes they mean well but simply don't show the respect they should for your needs or concerns, withholding money when you want to spend it on things that are really important to you but which they don't see the value in.

If you feel that you need to hand over control of your finances, doing so in a formal way will make you safer and give you a means of getting help if something goes wrong.

Putting someone else in charge of your finances

There are two different ways that you can formally hand control of your finances to another person (or more than one person).

The first is by ordinary power of attorney and the second is by lasting power of attorney (known as *continuing power of attorney* in Scotland and *enduring power of attorney* in Northern Ireland). You can only do this at a point where you can be legally recognised as having the mental capacity to make decisions, so you shouldn't wait until you're facing serious difficulties.

Ordinary power of attorney is a temporary, situational power that kicks in, for instance, when you go into hospital. You can set the terms and limits for it and choose whomever you wish to act on your behalf. You could choose a relative or a close friend because you think they know you best, or you could choose a solicitor because they will have no motive for acting against your expressed wishes and no risk of getting dragged into family feuds. Setting this up is simple and not prohibitively expensive for most people.

Lasting power of attorney (or the Scottish or Northern Irish equivalent) is a more serious matter because it applies indefinitely. In England and Wales, it has to be registered with the Court of Protection, and in Scotland with the Office of the Public Guardian; if you live in Northern Ireland, your chosen representative will have to apply to the High Court (Office of Care and Protection) at the point when you are no longer able to manage your own affairs. These institutions then have the duty to make sure that it is handled fairly. In England, Wales and Scotland, it doesn't have to kick in immediately – so, for instance, you can set it up to say that you will handle your own money until you lack the capacity to do so, at which point the person or people you have chosen will take over.

If you want, you can also give the person (or people) holding either type of power of attorney the right to make medical decisions on your behalf as well. (You can choose different people to make financial and medical decisions for you if you prefer.)

If you do this, you can change your mind about what you want at any time and let the solicitor who arranged the power of attorney know about it. The person representing you will then be legally obliged to take this into account when acting on your behalf.

8

Isolation in Later Life

One of the biggest worries many people have as they get older is that they will become isolated, especially if they experience increased difficulty in getting out and about. This is a still bigger problem for trans people, who are more likely to be estranged from family members and who have often lost friends in the process of transitioning. It can be compounded by anxiety about meeting new people, in case of rejection.

The internet has become a vital tool for many older people who are vulnerable to isolation, especially those who face difficulty getting around. Several charities and some financial institutions offer free support to help older people learn how to use technology and get online. You don't have to spend a lot of money on a computer – even a smartphone can suffice. If you really feel uncomfortable about technology, there are special tablet computers designed for people in your situation, with only a few functions which are easy to get the hang of. It's practically impossible to do anything with them that will make them go wrong.

Getting around

For many people, getting older means having poorer eyesight, slower reaction times and other problems that make it difficult or dangerous to drive. There's also a higher chance that you'll need to take medication of a sort that makes driving risky. For these reasons and more, many older people depend on getting lifts from friends or family members, or have to get around using public transport.

Trans people tend to have smaller networks of friends, and many – especially if they came out when awareness and understanding was poorer than it is today – have lost contact with some or all of their family members. This means they're all the more dependent on public transport in later life. For most this is not a problem, but for those who encounter hostility from drivers or other transport users, it can make life very difficult.

It's important to be aware that service providers – including the drivers of buses, trains and trams – are not allowed to discriminate against trans service users, who are protected by the Equality Act 2010. This means not only that it's unlawful for them to deny access to their vehicles, but that they are required to treat trans people with the same respect as their other passengers. If this doesn't happen, record the number and time of the service and report it to the organisation that runs the service. They will usually treat this type of complaint seriously and take action to ensure that you don't have any further problems.

Remember that getting older means you may be able to use some forms of public transport for free. Exactly what is available this way will depend on where you live.

Engagement in society

Even when getting around isn't a problem, some people shut themselves away as they get older because they don't feel valued and don't feel that they have anything useful to offer to society. This is a particular problem for people who have felt socially rejected in the past and those who suffer generally from low self-esteem.

It can be difficult to adjust post-retirement if most of your life has been centred around work. You'll suddenly find yourself with a lot more spare hours in the day, and this isn't always as much fun as it sounds. Work tends to shape our day-to-day routines, even if it's not our own work but that of a spouse or partner. When this changes, we need to find new routines and new ways of organising our time.

Often trans people are nervous about trying to make new friends because they don't want to encounter transphobia. Others find, however, that it's much easier to be natural around people once they're able to simply be themselves, and they make friends more easily as a result.

'I was sheltered and insecure before my transition. Now I'm outgoing and confident,' said Alyssa. '[I] had like a dozen close friends and around 100 Facebook acquaintances and now it's literally 10 to 20 times that.'

Some people find it difficult because they don't have good connections with other trans people and find that the friends they do have just don't understand the issues that they face because of their gender, while professional services are unable to provide adequate support. 'The only person that really understands when you're transgender is another transgender person,' says Gillian. 'The people at the gender clinic, they haven't really got a handle on it either. I think it's to do with money. They just haven't really got the money to support people like me. My wife left me, so I think for me the biggest challenge I've got is living the rest of my life with no partner and not that many close friends. I'm very isolated and vulnerable, you know?'

Kirsty has had a more positive experience. 'My social life is so much better post-transition than before,' she says. 'Simply as a result of being more comfortable in my own skin, I have more friends than before, plus the ones who were there before are still there. I have friends from within the trans community, the wider LGBTQ+[26] community and cis/hetero friends, none of whom I knew five years ago and many of whom I think will be friends for life. Oddly enough, the internet is more important for keeping in touch with longer-standing friends and family who have become more geographically dispersed over time. While I use the internet less to keep in touch with newer friends, sites like meetup.com have been really helpful in finding new people with similar interests.'

Religious activity

For many people, religious activity becomes more important with age, helping them to deal with issues like bereavement and their own mortality, as well as providing a supportive community. Increasingly, trans people are finding religious communities that welcome them, but because these are absent in many areas and travelling may become more difficult, it can be harder to maintain those connections.

For some people facing difficulties like this, online groups are helping to fill the void. They can help with fulfilling religious obligations and they can also act as signposts to local communities which are accepting and supportive. Being part of an online group means that even if you have a good local community, you'll never need to worry about being cut off due to health or disability issues or problems with transport or weather. During the Covid-19 lockdown, online groups became more organised and many say that they intend to carry on offering services like virtual mass or virtual iftar so that physically isolated people can still share these community events in future.

Searching online can also be a good way to get in touch with accepting religious communities which include people who are happy to help you with transport issues. For instance, many such groups make an effort to arrange to drive older people to services or ceremonies, or arrange home visits to make it easier to engage in shared activities.

Caregiving

Although we tend to think of older people as recipients of care, many are carers themselves. In England and Wales, over one and a quarter million people aged over 65 provide full-time care for somebody else.[27] Being a carer can be a very isolating experience, making it difficult to maintain friendships and even affecting casual social contact by making it hard to linger anywhere because of the cared-for person's needs.

If you're in this situation, it may be possible for you to arrange for respite care to be provided by your local council or a local charity, enabling you to get some time to yourself. Your GP's surgery can help you find contacts.

Bereavement

As we get older, our friends and loved ones get older too, and we inevitably experience more loss. This can be particularly difficult for trans people who have experienced rejection by friends and family members, and so have smaller social circles to begin with. Losing a partner is more difficult if you have lacked confidence in your ability to be loved, and complex feelings can arise around the death of a person you loved but were estranged from. It can also be difficult to deal with the death of a family member if other family members fail to respect your gender or simply don't want you around.

Different people vary greatly in their emotional reactions to bereavement, and these can be unpredictable. You may find yourself grieving in different ways for different individuals, which doesn't mean that your feelings for them were different or that they were any more or less important to you when they were alive. You may experience deep sadness, panic, anger or intense feelings of love, or you may not feel much at all. You may even feel relief, especially if death has brought suffering to an end. All of these reactions are natural but sometimes they can be hard to handle, especially in family situations that are already fraught.

At times like this, it's important to have people you can talk to, and it often really helps to talk to somebody who wasn't close to the deceased person and isn't going through this difficult emotional process at the same time. Not everybody knows how to cope in this situation, however, so try not to resent friends who seem a bit distant. If what you really want is just a hug and the chance to talk about something different, tell them so in plain terms and let them know that they don't need to be nervous around you.

Dealing with the death of a partner can be particularly traumatic if your partner's relatives don't recognise your relationship because you're trans. Where possible, this is a situation you should try to head off in advance by making careful arrangements for what happens after death (see Chapter 11), but some people find this upsetting in itself, and inevitably not everybody manages to make such arrangements in time. If you find yourself shut out of funeral arrangements, it's important to find your own way of saying goodbye. A separate memorial service, with people who knew and supported you both, and a visit to the place where your partner was buried or cremated can help to bring you closure.

If you're still finding it hard to cope with day-to-day life more than three months after a loved one's death, you may need professional grief counselling. This is most easily accessed privately, but if you're low on funds, then your GP may be able to help you get it through the NHS.

Sometimes, the death of a partner enables a trans person to begin expressing their true gender for the first time. Although this can be very liberating, there can also be feelings of guilt associated with having positive feelings after someone you love has died. It's important not to hide from these feelings but to work through them. Even if your partner didn't know that you were trans or felt unable to support you expressing your gender openly in public, they would probably want you to be happy now.

Reconciliation

Many trans people find that as they get older and their family members get older too, the desire to reconcile with parents or siblings who have kept their distance because of disputes around transition becomes stronger. Often, those people also experience a growing desire to find some sort of resolution before it's too late, even if they're not sure how to reach out. Because society has gradually become less transphobic (even if this isn't always apparent because committed transphobes make a lot of noise), it's quite common for relatives in this situation to feel less bothered by issues around transition than they used to. Realising that they made a mistake, however, they may then feel that there's no way to repair the relationship. This means that, in general, trans people who want to reconcile have to be the ones to make the first move, reaching out even at the risk of being rejected again.

Repairing a relationship is often easier with the aid of a third party. This could simply be a friend who promises to be there if it all goes wrong, or it could be a professional family counsellor. It's important to recognise that reconciliation won't always result in respect for a trans person's gender. Sometimes, however, simply being able to acknowledge continuing feelings of love and affection can help both parties, even if the conversation never gets any further than that. Similarly, it doesn't always mean staying in touch after reconnecting; simply having cleared the air can make people feel a lot better.

It's often the case that some family members will apologise for past rejection while others won't, or that some will respect the trans person's gender while others won't. This can make life complicated, but it's not insurmountable. The important thing is to make sure that the relatives who do try to be accepting understand that the behaviour of those who don't is distressing, and don't try to force everyone to spend time together in the hope that the tension will magically go away by itself. They need to recognise that nobody is under an obligation to put up with transphobia for the sake of togetherness, and that protecting trans people from this is part of what being accepting and supportive is about.

Sensory impairment

Some sensory deterioration is commonplace in old age. Seventy per cent of people over 70 have experienced hearing loss,[28] while 20 per cent of those over 75 have some degree of visual impairment.[29] There's a clear relationship between this kind of impairment and social isolation,[30] although it's difficult to determine the extent to which isolation is caused by this impairment as opposed to both being caused by other factors such as getting older. What we do know is that not being able to hear or see as well has a damaging effect on confidence, especially for those who are not part of communities of people in similar situations. This presents an intersectional risk for trans people who are already more likely than the average person to feel unsafe when out and about. There are also more subtle effects, such as feelings of uncertainty and embarrassment when not quite sure what's going on in a conversation – something that can be more difficult to shrug off if you've previously got into a habit of expecting bad reactions.

In most cases, sensory impairments develop slowly over time, and the best way to cope with them is to keep on doing as much as possible throughout this period. Getting help early also makes it easier to avoid their negative social impacts. This could mean getting glasses, contact lenses or a hearing aid, or it could simply mean talking to somebody from a support group to get advice on how to manage from day to day.

If you find yourself losing your hearing as you get older, you may be able to get help from your local Deaf community. Like all minority communities, the Deaf community can provide a strong sense of social support and a distinct cultural identity. Deaf people are bound together over time by shared experiences of perception and language, factors that have a profound effect on the way one understands and thinks about the world.

The flip side of being in such a community is that it increases the risks associated with social rejection. Although there are many openly trans and Deaf people out there, and although much of the Deaf community is supportive of trans rights, this may not be the case with every local community. Trans people may feel that there is nobody around like themselves, may struggle to find role models or may worry that they will be outright rejected, making it harder for them to find a supportive social environment.

Deaf people who routinely communicate in sign language usually learn their signing from their local community, as there is relatively little media content available that includes signing (and the majority of what exists is in American Sign Language (ASL) rather than British Sign Language (BSL) – there are significant differences). This means that they may lack the signs to talk about being transgender or non-binary, even if they are familiar with the written terms. Finger spelling can be used to work around this problem but it's comparatively slow and not well suited to situations like coming out, which can be highly emotive and prone to misunderstanding. One thing worth noting is that signed names don't always relate closely to names in English, and although some convey gender, not all do.

Sometimes people find it hard to sign as they get older, especially if they're not in the habit of doing so, because even minor arthritic conditions can make fingers stiff. This is an area where physiotherapy can be very effective, especially if it's started early on, before the problem has become severe. Ask your doctor if you can get a referral to your local physiotherapy department. If you have trouble getting out and about, they will be able to arrange for somebody to come and visit you at home.

Losing your hearing can make it harder to change the pitch of your voice. You can work around this by pressing two fingers against your Adam's apple and feeling the vibrations there. These will change when your voice is lower or higher, so you can practise this way and develop habits that will make it easier for you to blend in.

If you are losing your sight, it's useful to think about how you want to convey your gender through your appearance, now and as you get older. This will enable you to establish guidelines for any carers who assist you if the situation gets worse. Don't just think about clothes – think about things like wigs and facial hair as well. If you imagine that there will be a point when you want to go grey, is there a particular style of grey wig that you prefer? If you have a beard or are just starting to grow one post-transition, how will you want it to be shaped if you need somebody to trim it for you? If you want to wear make-up, pick out the shades that appeal to you.

Using the internet is incredibly important for many trans people as a means of accessing information and resources that are hard to find elsewhere, and as a means of finding community.

Using a screen reader and speech-to-text software means that this is still possible if you lose your sight, but it's much easier to learn how to use these tools if you make a start early, while you still have some useful vision. You may also want to get into the habit of using a recording device in situations where you might have a lot of information to remember, such as consultations with your doctor, especially if you are also beginning to find it harder to keep everything in your head.

Learning Braille is also an option if you are losing your sight, but only a minority of blind and visually impaired people use it, and it's not well supported. Some government leaflets about the practical aspects of transition are available in Braille, but unfortunately there are not many other resources for trans people in this format.

If you would like to have a guide dog to assist you, apply early, as it can take up to two years for a suitable animal to be available. If you are in the process of transition, this is something that you may want to discuss on application. Dogs are usually relaxed about their owners starting to take oestrogen, with many people reporting that they become more affectionate, but starting to take testosterone can lead to a male dog becoming uneasy and needing to re-establish who's boss.

Diet

Being on your own more can have knock-on effects, especially when it comes to eating. Many older people find that they depend more and more on convenience food because cooking becomes more difficult or no longer feels worthwhile. They're less likely to get the fresh fruit and vegetables that we all need to be healthy and maintain our energy levels. If this is a problem for you, there may be a local food service that can help you, or you may be able to take it in turns to cook for friends and have them cook for you. Simply talking about food in social media groups and sharing tips and recipes can help you to stay motivated, and if you feel more comfortable socialising with other trans people, you can find trans-focused forums where this kind of thing is welcomed. Looking after your diet can make a big difference to your ability to maintain your independence and find pleasure in life.

If you find it frustrating cooking single portions all the time, try cooking large amounts of foods like soup, stew or curry at once and freezing individual portions that you can heat up on future occasions. This is much healthier than relying on processed food. You may also find it useful to buy vegetables that remain good to eat after freezing, such as bell peppers and spinach.

Well-managed healthy eating can give you a sense of control over your body that helps to mitigate the stresses of dysphoria and ageing. It can also help to steady your hormone levels and your general metabolism, reducing your risk of mental health problems such as anxiety and depression, and improving the quality of your sleep – something that many people find deteriorates as they get older.

9

Trans and Non-Binary People Who Need Care

Most people eventually reach a stage in life when they struggle to take care of everything they need to for themselves. They might require help around the house, or with aspects of personal care at home, or they might need to consider moving into sheltered accommodation, a care home or a nursing home, where they can get more support. This can be daunting if you have had bad experiences with transphobia, but there are a lot of different options out there, and a lot of people who genuinely want to help you no matter who you are or how you live.

Day-to-day help

If you can still manage to look after yourself but there are a few things you need assistance with, you may be lucky enough to have friends or family members who can step in. Where this isn't the case, you may need to get the help of a cleaner, a gardener or an odd-job person – whatever is necessary to help you keep your surroundings in a condition that you're happy with.

If you're worried about letting strangers into your home because you've experienced abuse in the past and don't feel safe, ask your local LGBT society if they can recommend people they know will be respectful. You can also ask if anyone is willing to come and spend time with you while the helper is in your home, at least until you've had the chance to get to know them. Remember that anybody offering assistance on a professional basis is bound by the terms of the Equality Act 2010 and will be breaking the law if they discriminate against you because you're trans. The law also protects you from threats or harassment, and in Scotland any such behaviour clearly inspired by transphobia could constitute a hate crime.

Most people who need help like this on a regular basis soon get to know individuals they can trust, and good helpers can often recommend others for tasks that are outside their skill sets.

If you can't afford the help you need and it's impossible to manage without it, you may be able to get a home help paid for by your local council. This will usually be for just a few hours a week and you will only be able to ask them to do light tasks. If you think this is appropriate for you, contact your local social services department.

If you live with a partner who does a lot of extra things around the house because you can't manage, you may still be eligible for help. You partner will not automatically be expected to be able to cope with all the extra strain.

Personal care

If it's getting difficult for you to manage things like getting in and out of bed, getting dressed or bathing, you may find that assistive devices can make your life easier, but the chances are that sooner or later you will need help with personal care. You can arrange this privately, or your GP can refer you for an assessment (prioritised based on your level of need) so that care can be arranged through your local council.

The approach to care provision taken by different councils varies quite a bit. In some areas, you may find it difficult to get access to the same carer on a regular basis, so you may have to deal with a series of different people, which increases the risk of encountering prejudice. It is illegal for any carer to discriminate against you because you're trans, however, and if you report such an incident, it will be taken seriously.

If you come from a community in which it's traditional for community members to provide care for those who need it, you will need to work out whether or not you want to come out to the people who are looking after you. Depending on your stage of transition and the nature of the care you need, you might not have the option of keeping secrets. Even if that option *is* there, it might be bad for your mental health, and trying to ignore mental health issues in order to manage physical ones can cause trouble if stress builds up over time. In this situation, it's important to remember that other care options are available, and if you're worried about encountering transphobia, that views within your community are unlikely to be monolithic, even if they seem that way. In particular, younger people are significantly less likely to be prejudiced. You may be able to find traditional forms of support without having to go outside your community.

If you rely on your partner or a relative for care, it's important to make sure that you don't lose other positive aspects of your relationship as a result. There are several UK organisations that provide support and advice for carers, helping them with what can be a stressful job and signposting them to useful resources. You may also want to consider going through counselling together to help you restructure your relationship and learn how to avoid any build-up of resentment. If the person who cares for you also experiences physical infirmity, make sure that you have a back-up plan in case something goes wrong, and take the time to consider other long-term options.

If at any point you feel abused or neglected by your carer, it's important to be aware that you can get help. Many people feel trapped in situations like this because they feel that there's nowhere else they can turn for day-to-day support, and this can be a particular problem for trans people, who often have fewer friends and lower self-esteem to begin with. In fact, there is help available and it can be arranged very quickly if necessary. A good way to access it is to explain your situation to a doctor or healthcare worker. You can arrange to be alone with someone like this simply by saying that you have an intimate personal issue you want to talk about, and they will back you up so that your carer can't insist on staying in the room. Getting help doesn't have to mean ending all association with your carer – there is a range of options which you can discuss to work out what's best for you.

Adapting your home

Sometimes simple adaptations to your home can make it possible for you to retain your independence for a lot longer. An occupational therapist from your local social services department can visit your home to make an assessment and suggest changes that might help. Depending on your circumstances, your local council may be willing to meet the full cost of these or give you some money towards them. They could include things like a rail to help you navigate outdoor steps safely, a stairlift to help you get between floors in your house or a special moving seat to help you get in and out of the bath safely.

Other changes you can make to improve your safety at home include getting yourself on the priority list with your energy supply company. Anybody who is disabled or in fragile health can do this. Some companies offer free assessments to make sure that devices in your house are easy to use, and almost all will commit to giving people in your situation top priority in case of power cuts or similar issues. You may also be able to get help with winter fuel bills.

Sheltered accommodation

For those still able to take care of most of their own needs, sheltered accommodation can provide a good compromise between fully independent living and moving into a care home. It allows for more privacy, which many trans people prefer if they're uncertain about how they'll be treated by other residents, but it still makes it easier to socialise as and when you want to than living in your own home does. Crucially, it means that some back-up is quickly available if you have a fall or struggle with a task such as replacing a lightbulb. Some forms of sheltered accommodation also have shared dining facilities as an option for residents, with low-cost meals available for those who struggle to cook their own or who prefer to eat in company.

Living in sheltered accommodation is a bit like living in a village. It's about being part of a community, and often trans people who move into such spaces find that this initially means being gossiped about. Indeed, that's something that happens to any new arrival, but for those who have previously had to cope with a lot of transphobia, it can be daunting. You will have your own space, however, and will be free to come and go to the extent that your health allows. What's more, because a lot of people living in this situation are keen to make new friends in order to avoid becoming isolated themselves, it's often a much more accepting environment than it initially appears to be.

Choosing a care home

Care homes are often talked about as if they're places that people choose for their parents rather than themselves. This actually has more to do with marketing than reality – most people don't like to think about needing to make such a move until they really have no other choice. In most cases, people require this sort of support for physical reasons long before they lose the ability to make decisions for themselves (if, indeed, that ever happens). If you feel pressured by your children to go into a care home, make sure they respect your right to be part of the decision-making process.

Despite the fact that they are frequently youth-orientated, local trans and LGBT support groups can be very helpful when it comes to finding a care home where the staff have a respectful and supportive attitude towards trans and non-binary people. Under the terms of the Equality Act 2010, no care home is allowed to discriminate against you because you're trans unless it is doing so as a proportionate means to a legitimate end,[31] but naturally some places offer a warmer welcome than others and you may have additional concerns about what makes a place right for you. If you belong to an additional minority group – for instance, if you're Muslim or if you're autistic – you will need to find somewhere that not only accommodates your gender but can also be trusted as far as your other needs are concerned.

Transphobia in social care settings sadly remains a frequent occurrence, but it is far from ubiquitous, with a 2017 survey by Stonewall[32] finding that 29 per cent of all trans people accessing social services have experienced it within the past year. In other words, although you will need to be wary, you should not assume that you'll be treated badly wherever you go – it's worth taking the time to try to find somewhere better.

When choosing a home, ask what the staff turnover is like. In places where this is very high, you may find yourself having to deal with staff who have not received proper equalities training, which can lead to problems. A home where staff turnover is low tends to be better for all its residents because it allows you to form friendly relationships with the people looking after you.

Some care homes have a very brusque way of interacting with residents, and a clear set of rules about things like when the day starts and ends, which everybody is expected to conform to. This isn't necessarily a bad thing – some people find that having this kind of routine and structure in their lives really suits them, but others need homes that allow for more individual variation. This can be particularly important if, for instance, you have a sleep disorder or a health condition that varies a lot from day to day.

If you're worried about safety because of what happened in some care homes during the early stages of the Covid-19 pandemic, ask what each home's individual policy would be in the same situation. Think about what you would need in your room in order to be able to isolate there in relative comfort if necessary.

Care homes and shared spaces

One of the biggest differences between being in a care home and living independently (even in sheltered accommodation) is that it's pretty much impossible to avoid using shared spaces. This means having to deal with other residents who, initially, you'll know nothing about. Whether or not you find yourself accepted by these people and able to get along with them can make as big a difference to your experience as the attitude and conduct of the staff.

The good news is that care home staff are used to making introductions (talk to them first about how you want to be introduced) and almost every care home resident prefers to be on good terms with those around them, so they have an incentive to be nice. Sometimes, however, residents have impaired cognition or self-control (because of the effects of a stroke, for instance) and may behave in a distressed or hostile way. If you experience abuse for any reason, the staff have a duty to put your safety (including your mental and emotional well-being) first. In an extreme case, this may mean arranging for you and a problem resident to use shared spaces at different times. In most cases, however, hostile reactions are motivated by fear of the unknown (as much because you're new as because you're trans) and things settle down once it's clear that you don't pose a threat.

You should never feel that you are obliged to out yourself to other residents or that you have to answer all their questions. If they know that you're trans, they're more likely to be accepting if they're able to understand more about what that means, raising any personal concerns they may have and learning why some popular media myths should not be taken seriously. This doesn't mean, however, that it's your job to enlighten them. Whereas some trans people prefer to take the bull by the horns and hold a question-and-answer session shortly after moving in, others may prefer to ask that an experienced equalities trainer or a member of a local support group come in to talk to residents, making it less personal. Still others prefer to ignore the whole business and simply let people get to know them as individuals, which is usually enough to dispel any worries over time.

Even if you find that everyone in your new care home is friendly and nobody has an issue with your gender history, problems can still occur because of wider societal transphobia. For instance, residents may have visitors who are openly transphobic or who are uncomfortable about them sharing space with a trans person. They may watch television programmes with overtly transphobic content and not understand that these are making you uncomfortable, or take it seriously if they do. If you have problems like this, talk to the staff. If they don't understand how it's affecting you, try contacting your local LGBT society to see if they can send somebody in who can help you to explain.

Being a visibly trans or non-binary person in a care home can have positive effects for other residents. It often means that gay, lesbian and bisexual residents feel safer being open about their sexuality – if they see you being accepted, they stop worrying as much about being rejected themselves. Other people may find that it gives them the opportunity to rethink aspects of how they express their own gender, not necessarily because they are trans but because of all the smaller ways in which strict codes of gendered presentation and behaviour can clash with what individuals really want out of life.

Family issues

Because many trans people experience a breakdown in their relationships with family members, it's common to develop close bonds with people who are not related by blood or marriage but who are just as important as parents, siblings and children are to others. This makes it important to find a care home with a flexible visitor policy that doesn't restrict access to only those people traditionally thought of as family members. Some care homes operate one policy from day to day and another, stricter one when a resident is seriously ill, so if you want close friends to be able to be there for you when you're at your most vulnerable, make sure that this won't be a problem.

When you enter institutional care for the first time, it is, of course, important to make sure that staff have a record of your next of kin. What many people don't realise, however, is that next of kin can be anybody – they don't have to be blood relatives. If you can't think of anybody suitable, you can nominate a solicitor who will then act in accordance with instructions you have prepared in advance should you become unable to advocate for yourself.

If there have been rifts in your family because of your transition, you'll need to make sure that you can trust staff to avoid gossiping about who has been visiting, even to other visitors. Make sure they understand if there's anyone you'd prefer them to keep in the dark about your transition. They should be used to keeping secrets when necessary – for instance, in situations in which residents don't want their relatives to know that their health is getting worse. If you want to, you can also ask them to stop specific people from visiting you.

Keeping your gender history private in a care home

If you want to keep your gender history private in your care home, you will have a number of issues to consider. Depending on the type of support you need, you should be aware that it may not be possible for you to avoid staff knowing. In order to avoid negative reactions, it's generally best to come out to them straight away.

Talk to staff about procedures for managing medication. Because some trans men need medication that other residents will associate with women, and some trans women need medication that other residents will associate with men, having it handed to you in public carries a risk of being outed. If you store your medication in your own rooms, make sure there's somewhere you can do so discreetly. If you see this simply as part of the privacy that ought to be due to every patient, you might be surprised to learn how often it's overlooked.

If you have had vaginoplasty and find that you still need to dilate (which isn't necessary in all cases – your consultant will be able to advise you), then it will be much easier if you can arrange to have a room with a private bath.

'While I'm sure every effort would be made, to accommodate the general aspects of personal care within a social care environment for transgender people, there would be concerns (certainly on my part) regards perhaps the more intimate procedures for transgender women. I do wonder how that would tactfully, and with dignity, be achieved,' says Steph, echoing a common concern. In fact, care of this sort can be arranged, but not every carer is willing to do it. If you reach a point where you are not able to do it for yourself even after being helped into a bath and provided with a dilator, ask your doctor to help you access the support you need.

Some older trans people report that they have felt uncomfortable telling people they don't want to be open about their gender history because younger people, even if they agree to help, see it as a problematic political choice. To the people concerned, it's usually not political at all, not a matter of shame and not a rule that they think all other trans people should abide by – it's just not a very interesting aspect of who they are and they don't want to be expected to talk about it. They would rather just quietly get on with living their lives.

10

Gender, Transition and Dementia

The idea of losing touch with one's sense of identity as one gets older is frightening for anyone. For trans and non-binary people, there's an added complication. What if you forget that you've transitioned? What if you expect people to use your old pronouns or the only name you can remember for yourself is one you left behind long ago? And what if you find yourself presenting in your true gender but can't remember whether the environment in which you are presenting is accepting and safe?

Dementia is a progressive disease which effects a third of the UK population, so it's not realistic to give assurances that this will never happen. There are, however, techniques you can use to help you hold on to your identity and sense of security for as long as possible.

Recognising dementia

People with dementia generally cope better, and for longer, if they get the right support early on. What's more, this can empower them to make their own decisions about some aspects of their treatment rather than having everything decided by other people because their dementia is too advanced. This means that it's important not to put off getting help if you start to exhibit what could be symptoms of this type of illness.

Everybody has days when they're a bit scatterbrained or find it difficult to concentrate, but if this seems to be happening more often than usual, it could be a sign that something's wrong. You might also find that you're getting worse at organising things or you're losing track of plans. You may have mood swings and experience more intense emotions than usual, you may persistently find it difficult to find the word you want to use, or you may find that you're becoming forgetful. If you have symptoms like these, talk to your doctor or to a nurse at your local practice, who will be able to give you advice. It might turn out that you have a different type of problem, in which case they can set your mind at ease.

Not everybody with dementia deteriorates significantly during their remaining years and many continue to enjoy a good quality of life. Specialist nursing for people in this situation is improving all the time and scientists continue to make breakthroughs in the search for a cure. The more warning you have that you are developing the disease, the easier it will be for you to take control of your circumstances and find the right solution for you, whatever that is.

Coming out due to dementia

Keeping secrets when you're affected by dementia can be very difficult, even if you've managed to keep them throughout your life. This can mean that trans people reveal their gender inadvertently because it's too hard to maintain the constant pretence of being somebody else. People who are used to being open about their gender with a few people – such as a support group or a handful of close friends – can find it especially difficult to keep track of what to say when, and to whom.

The positive side of this is that as long as the people you're around know that you're suffering from dementia, you're unlikely to meet with a seriously hostile reaction. People may worry that you're confused and don't know what you're saying, but they'll usually put anything that clashes with their worldview down to the illness. It will take time for them to realise – if they ever do – that there is something more significant going on, and that's time they can use to adjust emotionally.

If this happens during the early stages of dementia, you may realise that you've slipped up but still be able to take control of the situation. If you decide that the time has come to be open, it's useful to talk about your past, and especially any previous activities you have undertaken in relation to being trans (such as talking to your doctor about it or attending a support group), so that people will understand that this isn't a conclusion you have reached about yourself after the dementia set in.

If you feel that you might be at risk if you accidentally come out due to your dementia – for instance, because you're living with relatives who are aggressively transphobic – you should seek out a solicitor and set up a power of attorney. This means that the solicitor will be able to make decisions on your behalf, in accordance with instructions you have given when your mind is still lucid. This can empower a solicitor to check up on your well-being and, if necessary, have you removed from the place where you are staying and make alternative care arrangements for you. If you feel that this is something that needs to happen straight away, tell a solicitor or your doctor and they will be able to help.

Dementia during transition

For people who are still in the process of going through transition, the idea of developing dementia can be additionally frightening because of the prospect that you won't be considered competent to complete the process. In many cases, this kind of worry is unfounded. If you already have a diagnosis of gender dysphoria and you've made all the big decisions about how you want to proceed, your doctor will help you to proceed as far as you safely can in the context of this or any other mental health problem. It's important not to hide things from your doctor because this could potentially put you in a dangerous situation. For instance, you might need help to keep track of changes in your medication before surgery or to deal with all aspects of caring for yourself during your recovery, even if you are deemed competent to consent to the surgery itself.

If you haven't yet been diagnosed with gender dysphoria, your doctors will need to know about any other mental health problems you have in order to be sure that the diagnosis is made properly and you get the right help. If, for instance, you start taking hormones and experience severe mood swings, a doctor who doesn't know that you have already been having problems of this type due to possible undiagnosed dementia might think that they are caused by the hormones and stop prescribing them, rather than looking for better ways of managing your treatment.

Early-stage dementia and transitioned people

If you have gone through a full binary transition before you develop dementia, you will need to think about how this could affect your future care and make sure that the right protections are in place going forward. There are several issues to consider:

- If you end up being moved between doctors, a future doctor might not realise why you are taking hormones. This will need to be made very clear in your medical notes so that there's no danger of them being stopped at a point when you are unable to understand why you need them yourself, or unable to advocate for yourself.

- If you are cared for or given medical treatment in places where you are not known, there's a possibility that nobody will realise you are trans, which could result in you missing out on some of the help you need or getting the wrong type of treatment. Discuss this with care professionals early on so a plan can be put in place.

It can be a good idea to discuss your concerns with a solicitor at this stage. You can then draw up a set of instructions – with as many explanatory notes as you want for those expected to act on them – which your solicitor can draw on to ensure that you're treated appropriately. Most solicitors are used to dealing with people who are suffering from early-stage dementia and they will go over things carefully with you to make sure that everything is clear. Unlike family members, they won't let their own or other people's feelings or beliefs affect what they do – they will be solely concerned with representing you.

When researching for this book, it was clear that, of all the issues associated with getting older, dementia was the one that worried trans people the most.

'I would worry that it would cause confusion and distress in my own mind if I couldn't remember social transition or surgery (expected late this year or early next),' said Kirsty. 'I might go into a male toilet and try to use a urinal. I might even stop responding to my name and revert to using my deadname. It's upsetting to imagine a future version of myself who can only recognise the old version of me. My urge to be feminine has been there since a very young age, dressing up in secret, etc. I would hate to think that in old age I might think that it's a shameful secret again, after taking years to get out of the closet.'

Dementia and control of your gender expression

Regrettably, some trans people with dementia find themselves at the mercy of family members who do not respect their gender. Whether they are cared for directly by those family members or placed in a care home where the staff are told not to let them express their gender, they can be denied hormone treatment and can find themselves effectively forced to detransition, which can cause severe dysphoria. The sense of gender is deep-rooted and tends to remain for a long time even after awareness of other aspects of life and identity has begun to fade.

As noted above, talking to a solicitor and giving power of attorney to them or to a trusted friend can protect you from ending up in that situation, as it allows your pre-established instructions to take precedence over your family's wishes. You can ask the person with power of attorney to check up on your living situation and arrange to have you moved if necessary. You will always be entitled to a place in a state care home, even if you have relatives who are offering to look after you, and care home staff are obliged by the Equality Act 2010 to respect your gender. Even though this cannot provide you with complete protection, it can make you a lot safer.

Appropriate care

Caring for somebody with dementia is difficult, and additional complications can arise where trans people are concerned, even when carers are respectful and well intentioned. For instance, group activities for dementia patients often revolve around sharing early memories – the ones likely to remain clear for longest – which can be distressing for people who endured a lot of transphobia in their youth or who simply find it hard to reconcile those memories with who they are now. It's a good idea for carers in this situation to get to know trans people they support one-to-one first and work out how best to approach such matters on an individual basis.

As dementia progresses, some trans people become confused about what gender role they are living in and how others see them. This can mean that, for instance, a trans man who still becomes dysphoric if he doesn't get testosterone suddenly begins to worry about his beard and body hair, or feels uncomfortable with a male carer dressing him. It's important for carers to be aware of this possibility and work closely with patients to provide the best support they can, adjusting it over time as required.

'I would require additional support and reassurance if I were to be cared for as Sophie,' explained one trans woman, who transitioned in her 40s. 'I am due to have lower surgery. This would be significant if an illness such as dementia made me forget that. And also breast development. I wouldn't have issues with my internal feelings as they have been constant throughout my life, but for some, gender dysphoria develops later in life.'

People with dementia frequently forget to take their medication, and where trans people are concerned, this includes hormones, potentially resulting in severe dysphoria, anxiety and even suicidal ideation. It's important for carers to ensure that this doesn't happen. When people are living alone in the early stages of the disease, mobile phone reminder apps can be a useful tool, especially if used in conjunction with pill boxes which make it easy for them to check the date.

Keeping confidences

Most trans people have quite a few trans friends, and if those people are not open about their trans status, either because they have never come out or because they transitioned a long time ago and now never talk about their pre-transition history, that means that it's important to keep their secrets. This can become difficult to do when living with dementia, which is a big worry for some people.

If you're concerned that you might breach friends' confidences, it's best to be up front with them about it so that they have some warning. This gives them the chance to figure out how they would respond if you inadvertently put them in a difficult situation. It also means that, if you want to, you can give them permission to dismiss what you've said by stressing that you're confused. Some people hesitate to do this without permission because it makes them feel guilty.

Some dementia sufferers deal with this sort of situation by deciding early on to start telling wild and unlikely stories about all sorts of people, thus decreasing the chance that any one story will be taken seriously. This isn't for everyone, as it can make it harder to get people to accept what you have to say when you're being sincere, but if your stories are entertaining, then you may find that it gives you a new, positive way of engaging with people that's easier than having to rely on a shaky memory.

11

Wills and Funeral Planning

Getting one's affairs in order becomes more and more important in later life. It's especially important for trans and non-binary people who have complicated family lives or are estranged from some family members. Plans need to be put in place so that it's clear what should be done if declining health means an individual can no longer make their own decisions, so that it's clear what they want to happen to their estate in the event of death and so that funeral providers know how they wish to be remembered.

Power of attorney

If you don't have contact with your next of kin or you don't have a positive relationship with them, you may be worried about the way decisions could be made on your behalf if you become incapable of making them for yourself. This could be because you gradually lose control of your faculties over time due to an illness like dementia or it could be because of a sudden crisis such as a stroke. As these risks increase in later life, it's a good idea to take measures to ensure that there will be someone who can make decisions in accordance with your wishes.

The easiest way to do this is to grant power of attorney, effectively putting somebody else in the position that your next of kin would be otherwise. This could, for instance, be a long-term partner who is otherwise at risk of being overridden by family members if you haven't married. It could be a best friend who knows you better than anybody else in the world. There's also the option of nominating a solicitor for this role, and because they don't have an emotional stake in proceedings, solicitors are in fact often the best choice.

If you choose a solicitor, you won't be able to rely on them knowing automatically what your wishes in any given situation would be. In fact, whoever you choose, it's a good idea to leave clear, written instructions in an obvious place. These can cover things like who should be allowed to visit you and, if your health severely deteriorates, under what circumstances you would like life support to be withdrawn. Importantly, they can also cover what gender you wish to be recognised as, what name and pronouns should be used for you, and a range of other issues such as what sort of clothes you should be dressed in if you're unable to dress yourself. There is not normally any additional charge associated with the length of the instructions you leave, so write in as much detail as you can.

The process of setting up power of attorney is simple. Although you might need to save up for it if you're struggling on a state pension, it's financially within reach of almost everyone, and there are charities you can turn to for help if it's not. If you have trouble getting out and about, you shouldn't have difficulty finding a solicitor who will be willing to come to your home at no extra charge.

Leaving a legacy

Most older people who have children, grandchildren or nephews and nieces (or *niblings*, as the non-binary offspring of siblings are increasingly called) want to leave something to them after they die, even if the relationship is not a close one. You may also have a partner or spouse and want to make sure that they're properly provided for.

Leaving a legacy is about more than just writing a will. From a financial perspective, it could be about setting up a trust fund or rearranging your finances so that less of what you hope to pass along is taxed. Looked at another way, it can mean things like writing special messages or making videos for your loved ones to enjoy after you're gone. Some people even choose to wrap gifts. This approach can reinforce the sense of personal connection and love even after somebody has died, and help survivors to get through the grieving process.

Making a will

Making a will is much simpler – and quite a bit cheaper – than most people expect. At its most basic, this document will simply explain who should get what if you die, and there's room for some flexibility in the wording – for instance, you might say that you want to leave your daughter half of your money (you don't need to specify how much that is); or that you want to leave your brother all of your furniture (you don't need to list it item by item). This simple structure means that most wills stand for a considerable period of time without needing to be updated. You will need to arrange an update, however, if you go through a major life change such as getting married or divorced, buying or selling a house, or having a child. It's a good idea to change it if you transition in order to make sure that all the language is correct, but this won't usually affect anything substantial.

'I already had a will pre-transition so it was just a matter of changing this slightly,' said Kirsty. 'My solicitor also dealt with my divorce which was caused by my transition so was/is well aware of it. It's only a small practice in Northern Ireland but it honestly never occurred to me to expect any negative reaction from them, and they were fine. I am generally more apprehensive dealing with large faceless companies where I might not fit in with their standard expectations; I feel pretty comfortable with smaller businesses where I feel treated as an individual. I'm also pretty lucky in that I haven't lost any friends or family as a result of my transition – my brother and sister are executors of my will and also trustees should I die before my kids reach maturity.'

Once you have a basic will in place, adding to it is simple. If you want your more detailed requests to be legally enforceable, you will need to get them witnessed by your solicitor. If you do this when making a new will, it won't cost you anything extra. If you simply want to leave new instructions that you trust your potential heirs to go along with, you can write them down and send them to your solicitor at any time, asking that they be added to your will. They will then be referenced when the will is read out after your death.

In the absence of a will, a close relative will usually be given the legal right to manage your estate and decide what goes where. If you have been cohabiting with a partner you are not legally married to, there is no guarantee that your partner will be able to assume this role.

If you have no living relatives, a solicitor will normally be appointed to manage your estate.

Funeral planning

These days, most funerals are conducted in very similar ways, and people organising them often report that they don't feel they have much control over the process. Although this makes it easier for some, it can be an issue for people who have complex family issues to work around or special concerns about how they are presented – both of which are more common for trans people.

The good news is that there are funeral directors out there who are prepared to listen and to take a more individual, person-centred approach. If you do your research and find a few good options in advance of them being needed, this can make things much easier for your executor – especially if that person is a loved one who is likely to be dealing with grief after you die and who may therefore feel less capable of standing up for what you wanted. Funeral directors like this will usually be happy to meet and discuss options with you.

Once you have made a funeral plan and recorded all the details in writing, you can ask your solicitor to add it to your will. This usually costs very little to do.

Having a funeral plan isn't just about ensuring that you are respected after death. If you have a surviving partner or close friends, it can be very important to them to see that you are treated respectfully, especially at a time when they are having to deal with grief. Leaving clear instructions in the hands of a neutral person removes much of the potential for conflict between your chosen family and any relatives who are hostile about your transition. If some of your friends are themselves visibly trans, it can make it safer for them to attend your memorial service.

Misgendering after death

One of the big fears many trans people have is that, after they die, relatives will 'reclaim' their old gender, reinstating old names and pronouns, and erase any history of transition. Not only is it distressing to think of being misrepresented like this, especially by people who may have been directly transphobic when one was alive, it can also cause distress to friends and other family members who have no control over the situation.

If you're concerned that this may happen to you, there are several things you can do about it:

- Give social media profiles to trusted friends so they can preserve your identity there.

- Contribute to trans history projects like those connected with the Oral History Society[33] so that your story will form part of a collection for posterity.

- Arrange for a solicitor to ensure that your correct name and gender are used on official documents.

Despite what some people believe, it is not necessary for a person to hold a gender recognition certificate in order for them to be registered as the gender they normally live in at the time of death, as long as that gender is either male or female.

Sometimes bodies have to be identified quickly – for instance, in the event of several people being killed in an accident – and it is not possible for the coroners dealing with them to get help from solicitors or relatives straight away. In this case the wrong gender can be used and can be difficult to amend. Coroners[34] and their staff routinely check documents found on the body, such as drivers' licences or library cards, to determine gender if it is otherwise unclear. This means that it's a good idea to carry something with your name and gender on it or, if you have only recently come out and don't feel ready to express your gender this way, carry a card that specifically directs medical personnel (including those who deal with dead bodies) to contact a doctor or solicitor who can explain your situation.

If you cross-dress or are going through a process of exploring your gender but you would actually prefer to have your death registered under your birth gender, it's still useful to leave clear instructions, just in case your presentation at the time of your death leads to confusion.

If you are non-binary, you won't be able to have that registered on your death certificate, but you will be able to leave instructions about what pronouns should be used for you and how your body should be presented after your death. You may want to leave specific instructions for the funeral director to explain how your gender fitted in with other aspects of your life, because they may not always be sure of the best way to reflect this aspect of your life.

If your body is going to be embalmed, it's important that there is clarity about your gender right away, so that the embalmer knows how you prefer to be presented. If you're non-binary, morticians may not be sure of the best way to proceed, so it's best to leave quite specific instructions. If some of your loved ones don't know that you're trans or if you're in a situation where you present yourself differently to different groups of people, you will have to think carefully about how you would prefer your body to be presented. Most people facing this situation aim to strike a balance between being true to themselves and minimising any additional difficulties for mourners (who may, for instance, be faced with explaining why you didn't want to come out to some people when you were alive).

Although they're getting better at this, morticians don't always have a good understanding of trans issues, so it's important to make sure that there are adequate instructions – or somebody speaking on your behalf – to explain to them that your gender is as you have stated it, regardless of how your body may appear to them and regardless of whether or not you have a gender recognition certificate. Most morticians do their best to correctly interpret the wishes of the deceased because, alongside their natural desire to respect their clients, they know that their professional reputations depend on it.

If you depend on special clothing or accessories, such as a wig or a binder, to express your gender, you may want to make this explicit in your instructions about how your body is to be presented. You should also leave instructions as to where these items can be found in case you're not wearing them when you die.

12

What Older Trans People Have to Give

When, as a society, we're used to thinking about older people in terms of their needs, and when we see trans people as a vulnerable group, it's easy to overlook what older trans people have to offer. In fact, their enhanced awareness of gender means that they can provide valuable insights into the changes that have taken place in society over the past few decades, and how those changes have affected ordinary people. Many can also help us to understand the development of the LGBT rights movement and social justice movements more widely.

Gender in history

Most people grow up assuming that the gender roles they see around them, the ones they're expected to follow, are normal and natural. For many trans people, there is an awareness that something is amiss which develops very early in life. Sociologists and anthropologists, aware of how much these roles vary between cultures, can examine their impact academically, but trans people study them from childhood, like embedded ethnologists, and observe the way they change throughout their lives. This means that by the time they reach old age they carry a tremendous amount of knowledge about matters that are just background noise to most others.

Drawing on this understanding makes it easier to bridge the divide between an academic view of history and real human experience. It provides a useful adjunct to the narratives provided by cis women who recall instinctively rebelling against their narrow social roles from early childhood. These perspectives help to inform efforts to counter regressive social trends, and thereby help to ensure the protection of hard-won rights, keeping us on course towards building a more equal society in the future.

LGBT rights and social justice

When one has a sexual orientation or gender experience that doesn't match social norms, it's never easy to live in secret, even if being open is dangerous. For many trans people, however, it has simply never been *possible* to live in secret. Older trans people often describe being the subject of adult anxiety when, as children, they strayed outside the bounds of their approved gender roles without understanding what the social impact of this could be. Others found that, even as adults, they simply didn't have the acting skills to convince as the gender they were expected to be, and without access to puberty blockers and early hormone treatment, the majority were never able to 'pass' when simply trying to be themselves. As a result, they frequently found that they had no alternative but to stand up and fight for their rights, and they were often to be found at the forefront of LGBT rights campaigning.

This involvement in pivotal movements within LGBT history means that many trans people have extensive campaigning skills they can share with subsequent generations. Sharing personal stories can help to embolden younger people and give them the confidence they need to overcome structural barriers.

Personal matters

Alongside all this, older trans people play important roles in our communities. Many are parents, spouses, partners, siblings, friends. Being treated as outsiders has taught them strong community-building skills and they appreciate the value of loyalty and mutual support more than most people. Whether or not they are also dependent on support, they have a lot to contribute to society.

13

Closing Notes

Getting older always comes with challenges but it can also be a rewarding experience, a process of feeling more and more at ease with one's own identity, and this is no different for trans and non-binary people. Although prejudice and discrimination continue to present huge difficulties, society overall is much more accepting than it was a few decades ago, and many older trans people say that they feel they have found a place in the world that they never had before.

Geographic location, class and ethnic background are major factors in the unevenness of trans people's experiences. Major metropolitan areas tend to offer much better services and support, although there are exceptions, with some older trans people reporting that they are happily settled in villages with friendly and respectful neighbours. Economic hardship makes older trans people vulnerable by leaving them dependent on state services of highly variable quality, but those with money are usually able to access support and establish living arrangements in which transphobia is rarely a problem. This illustrates that it is possible to provide a more positive experience for all older trans people – what is needed is the institutional and political will to make it happen.

It's easy to put the focus on transphobia when looking at the challenges faced by older trans and non-binary people, but it's important to remember that ageism is also an issue, and that prejudice against older people, as well as a frequent failure to cater for their needs which often happens simply because they haven't been given enough thought, also complicates their lives. This can be a particular issue within the LGBT community, where social opportunities are more often geared towards young people and venues are often difficult to access for those with limited mobility (often just as a consequence of upstairs spaces being cheaper and niche organisations having limited funds).

Provision for trans men and trans women remains much better overall than that available to non-binary people, largely because the latter group still lacks official recognition in most contexts. Each of these groups experiences different kinds of prejudice and discrimination, and people working to support them need to be aware of this.

Getting older often prompts people to look back on their lives and think about what they have missed out on. 'When I think of all the years of my life that have been wasted on dysphoria, I just think, imagine how productive I could have been!' said Eleanor. Yet just as experiences like this can be used to illustrate the damage done by social exclusion and policy failures, they can also help to inform strategy development in the present day, making sure that younger trans people – and members of other minority groups – will not have to endure the same difficulties.

It's also possible to focus on the positive. Many older trans people see themselves as survivors. As part of a population with high rates of suicide and illness, some did not expect to reach old age. Where their peers worry about the advancing years, they are grateful for the time they've had and enjoy having reached a stage in life when some things become easier.

'One of the things that's becoming increasingly important to me is to reassure people,' said Jo. 'To say, look, it's all right. It's all right being trans, it's all right getting old and it's all right being non-binary. All these things which, I mean, gosh, used to worry me, all that stuff is going away.'

Appendix 1: Finding Out More

Where can you find out more about supporting older trans people? The following organisations can provide advice and support.

Information, research and training to help you understand trans people's lives

GIRES – the Gender Identity Research & Education Society collates research on important issues concerning trans people and can provide advice on best practice.

www.gires.org.uk

The Scottish Trans Alliance – a charity supported by the Scottish government which carries out research, provides training and has an extensive collection of resources that can help you to understand many different aspects of trans people's lives.

www.scottishtrans.org

Stonewall – a charity focused on LGBT rights which carries out research on trans people's experiences, and provides training.

www.stonewall.org.uk

Information on trans people in healthcare environments

NHS England has its Gender Dysphoria Protocol on its website with help for healthcare professionals who need to refer patients to specialist gender services, plus information for GPs on how to prescribe and monitor hormones.

https://actiononhearingloss.org.uk/information-and-support/support-for-health-and-social-care-professionals/communication-tips-for-healthcare-professionals – see Appendix A.

NHS Scotland has its Gender Reassignment Protocol on its website along with explanatory notes and additional guidance for healthcare professionals.

www.ngicns.scot.nhs.uk/nhs-scotland-gender-reassignment-protocol-grp

NHS Wales details how trans patients should be supported in its Specialised Services Policy (CP21), which is available on its website.

www.whssc.wales.nhs.uk/document/281109

Information for older trans people who need social and practical support

Age UK has a good reputation for understanding and supporting trans people. It runs an advice line and befriending service, organises social activities for older people and provides a list of people who can help with odd jobs.

www.ageuk.org.uk

Appendix 2: Glossary of Terms

Most people reading this book will find that it contains quite a bit of unfamiliar language. This glossary provides an easy way to check any words you're uncertain about, both in the book itself and in your day-to-day contact with trans and non-binary people.

agender *adj*. Having no gender, being outside the system of gender.

androgyne *adj., n*. (Person) having qualities of maleness and femaleness; usually used to refer to presentation.

autogynephilia *n*. The theoretical state whereby a heterosexual man is sexually excited by imagining or presenting himself as female.

bigender *adj*. Having qualities of maleness and femaleness; used to refer to presentation or identity.

binary transgender *adj*. Pertaining to a man who was categorised as female at birth or a woman who was categorised as male at birth.

binary transition *np*. The process of transitioning from male to female or from female to male.

binder *n*. A garment worn by trans men and some non-binary people to flatten the chest area and reduce the appearance of breasts.

bottom surgery *np*. Surgery to change the appearance of the genitals, carried out as part of transition.

cis *adj*. Having a gender identity consistent with the way one was categorised at birth; short for *cisgender*.

cis man *np*. A man who was categorised as male at birth.

cis woman *np*. A woman who was categorised as female at birth.

cisgender *adj*. Having a gender identity consistent with the way one was categorised at birth.

cross-dress *v.* To wear clothing normally associated with a different gender; especially to dress in female-associated clothing if male.

deadname *n., v.* A personal name no longer used by a trans person, usually because of its association with the wrong gender; to call or refer to a person by such a name.

detransition *v., n.* To reverse the social, hormonal or surgical aspect of a transition from one gender role to another; the process of undertaking such a reversal.

DSD *np.* An acronym meaning *disorders of sexual development* or *differences of sexual development* and referring to intersex variations.

dysphoria *n.* The state of feeling deeply uneasy or dissatisfied with life. Frequently used by trans people in reference to *gender dysphoria*.

fa'afafine *n.* A person from Samoa who is transfeminine and has a specific cultural role.

gender confirmation surgery *np.* A collective term for surgeries used to make a person's body more accurately reflect their gender; also, a term used to refer specifically to surgery used to make a person's genitals more accurately reflect their gender.

gender dysphoria *np.* The state of feeling deeply uneasy or dissatisfied with the gender role one is living in.

gender reassignment surgery *np.* Another term for *gender confirmation surgery*, now considered archaic and somewhat inaccurate.

genderfluid *adj.* Experiencing different internal genders at different times; presenting in differently gendered ways at different times.

genderqueer *adj., n.* Having a gender identity that is not wholly or consistently male or female; a person whose gender identity is neither wholly nor consistently male or female.

hermaphrodite *adj., n.* Being born with a body which does not meet typical expectations of maleness or femaleness, or spontaneously developing a body which does not meet typical expectations of maleness or femaleness in adolescence; a stigmatising term which some people are trying to reclaim.

hijra *n.* A person from the Indian subcontinent who is either intersex or transfeminine and has a specific cultural role.

intergender *adj.* Having a gender identity that is between male and female.

intersex *adj.* Being born with a body which does not meet typical expectations of maleness or femaleness, or spontaneously developing a body which does not meet typical expectations of maleness or femaleness in adolescence.

mangina *n.* A trans man's vagina; a term sometimes used to reduce dysphoria when discussing genitals.

misgender *v.* To use incorrectly gendered pronouns or adjectives when describing somebody.

Mx *n.* A non-gendered title equivalent to Mr or Ms.

neutrois *adj.* Identifying as neutrally gendered, neither male nor female.

non-binary *adj.* Having a gender identity that is not wholly or consistently male or female; having a gender identity that is neither wholly nor consistently male or female. An inoffensive umbrella term for genders that are neither male nor female.

Per *n.* A non-gendered title equivalent to Mr or Ms.

polygender *adj.* Having aspects of multiple genders.

retransition *v., n.* To undertake the process of transition again after having detransitioned; the process of going through a transition after having done so at least once previously.

shemale *n.* A person who has a penis and breasts; this term usually refers to someone who was categorised as male at birth. It is highly stigmatising and associated with pornography and sex work.

TERF *n.* An acronym for *trans exclusive radical feminist*, referring to a person (usually female) who identifies as a radical feminist and does not recognise trans women as women.

top surgery *np.* Surgery carried out on the chest area, usually to enhance, reduce or remove breasts.

tranny *n.* A trans woman or a transvestite. This is a heavily stigmatising term associated with pornography and sex work, but there is a significant movement to reclaim it for the purposes of self-identification.

trans *adj.* Short for *transgender* but frequently used on its own where the context is clear.

trans man *np.* A man who was categorised as female at birth.

trans woman *np.* A woman who was categorised as male at birth.

transfeminine *adj.* Descriptive of a trans woman or a non-binary person who leans in the direction of a feminine identity or presentation.

transgender *adj.* Having a gender identity inconsistent with the way one was categorised at birth; this term is also used in a narrower sense to refer specifically to people who have gone through a binary transition.

transgenderism *n.* An ideological position supportive of trans rights; this term is primarily used by people opposed to trans rights and should not be considered politically neutral.

transition *v., n.* To undergo the psychological, social, hormonal or surgical process of moving from life in one gender role to life in another; the undertaking of the psychological, social, hormonal or surgical process of moving from life in one gender role to life in another.

transmasculine *adj.* Descriptive of a trans man or a non-binary person who leans in the direction of a masculine identity or presentation.

transmisogyny *n.* Intersectional prejudice faced by trans women which combines elements of transphobia and misogyny.

transphobia *n.* Prejudice against trans people.

transsexual *adj.* A person who is transitioning or has transitioned from male to female or from female to male. This term is sometimes considered inappropriate because it leads to easy confusion between gender and sexual orientation.

transvestite *n., adj.* A person who cross-dresses.

Pronouns

Several alternative pronouns are used by non-binary people in place of *he*, *she* and their derivatives. The following table details some of the most common ones, with more familiar examples to provide context.

Nominative	Accusative	Possessive adjective	Possessive pronoun	Reflexive
he	him	his	his	himself
she	her	her	hers	herself
they	them	their	theirs	themselves*
zie	zie	zir	zirs	zirself
xe	xe	xir	xirs	xirself
sie	hir	hir	hirs	hirself
per	per	per	pers	perself
fae	faer	faer	faers	faerself
co	co	co	cos	coself
ey	em	eir	eirs	emself

* Sometimes when *they* is used as a singular pronoun, the reflexive form *themself* is preferred.

The linguistic terms here might sound confusing but these pronouns are easy to use in practice. These examples show how the elements in the above table can be applied in simple sentences:

Nominative: There *she* is.

Accusative: Look at *her*.

Possessive adjective: That's *her* stick.

Possessive pronoun: That stick is *hers*.

Reflexive: She chose that stick for *herself*.

Endnotes

1   *William and the Werewolf*, translated from the French *Guillaume de Palerme* by William, 1350; *The Wycliffe Bible*, 1382 (Ecclesiasticus).

2   Ulrichs, K.H. (1898) *Forschungen über das Rätsel der mannmännlichen Liebe* [Research on the Mystery of Male–Male Love]. Leipzig: Max Spohr.

3   'Ex-GI becomes blonde beauty.' *New York Daily News*, 1 December 1952.

4   Feinberg, L. (1996) *Transgender Warriors: Making History from Joan of Arc to Dennis Rodman*. Boston, MA: Beacon Press.

5   Park, A., Bryson, C., Clery, E., Curtice, J. and Phillips, M. (eds) (2013) *British Social Attitudes 30*. London: NatCen Social Research, p.115. Accessed on 26/06/2020 at www.bsa.natcen.ac.uk/media/38723/bsa30_full_report_final. pdf.

6   It's a sad irony that government AIDS-awareness posters produced during this decade bore the slogan 'Don't die of ignorance'.

7   Ho, V. (2019) 'Pioneer of gender-reveal party regrets sparking trend: "Let kids be who they are".' *The Guardian*, 27 July. Accessed on 26/06/2020 at www.theguardian.com/culture/2019/jul/26/gender-reveal-party-pioneer-regrets-trend.

8   Jenness, V., Maxson, C., Matsuda, K.N. and Sumner, J.M. (2007) *Violence in California Correctional Facilities: An Empirical Examination of Sexual Assault*. Irvine, CA: Center for Evidence-Based Corrections, University of California, Irvine. Accessed on 26/06/2020 at https://ucicorrections.seweb. uci.edu/files/2013/06/PREA_Presentation_PREA_Report_UCI_Jenness_et_ al.pdf.

9   Clements-Nolle, K., Marx, R. and Katz, M. (2006) 'Attempted suicide among transgender persons: The influence of gender-based discrimination and victimization.' *Journal of Homosexuality 51*, 3, 53–69. doi: 10.1300/ J082v51n03_04.

10 Jackman, K.B., Dolezal, C., Levin, B., Honig, J.C. and Bockting, W.O. (2019) 'Stigma, gender dysphoria, and nonsuicidal self-injury in a community sample of transgender individuals.' *Journal of Psychiatric Research 269*, 602–609. doi: 10.1016/j.psychres.2018.08.092.

11 Diamond, M. (2013) 'Transsexuality among twins: Identity concordance, transition, rearing, and orientation.' *International Journal of Transgenderism 14*, 1, 24–38. doi: 10.1080/15532739.2013.750222.

12 'Transgender no longer recognised as "disorder" by WHO.' BBC News, Health, 29 May 2019. Accessed on 26/06/2020 at www.bbc.co.uk/news/health-48448804.

13 Turban, J.L., Beckwith, N., Reisner, S.L. and Keuroghlian, A.S. (2019) 'Association between recalled exposure to gender identity conversion efforts and psychological distress and suicide attempts among transgender adults.' *JAMA Psychiatry 77*, 1, 68–76. doi:10.1001/jamapsychiatry.2019.2285.

14 'Germany's Cabinet approves ban on gay, transgender "conversion therapy".' *Deutsche Welle*, 18 December 2019. Accessed on 26/06/2020 at www.dw.com/en/germanys-cabinet-approves-ban-on-gay-transgender-conversion-therapy/a-51717750; Bulman, M. (2019) 'Justin Trudeau moves forward with ban on LGBT+ conversion therapy across Canada.' *The Independent*, 14 December. Accessed on 26/06/2020 at www.independent.co.uk/news/world/americas/canada-ban-conversion-therapy-lgbt-trudeau-a9247136.html.

15 Bauer, M., Truffer, D. and Plattner, K. (2014) *Intersex Genital Mutilations: Human Rights Violations of Children with Variations of Sex Anatomy*. NGO Report to the 2nd, 3rd and 4th Periodic Report of Switzerland on the Convention on the Rights of the Child. Accessed on 28/07/2020 at http://intersex.shadowreport.org/public/2014-CRC-Swiss-NGO-Zwischengeschlecht-Intersex-IGM_v2.pdf.

16 Gouze, K.R. and Nadelman, L. (1980) 'Constancy of gender identity for self and others in children between the ages of three and seven.' *Child Development 51*, 1, 275–278.

17 Gülgöz, S., Glazier, J.J., Enright, E.A., Alonso, D.J. *et al.* (2019) 'Similarity in transgender and cisgender children's gender development.' *Proceedings of the National Academy of Sciences of the United States of America 116*, 49, 24480–24485. doi: 10.1073/pnas.1909367116.

18 Young, A. (2001) *Women Who Become Men: Albanian Sworn Virgins*. Oxford: Berg Publishers.

19 Stonewall (2017) *LGBT in Britain: Hate Crime and Discrimination*. London: Stonewall, pp.16–19. Accessed on 26/06/2020 at www.stonewall.org.uk/system/files/lgbt_in_britain_hate_crime.pdf.

20 Crisp, Q. (2017) *The Last Word: An Autobiography*. San Diego, CA: MB Books.

21 Zimman, L. (2019) 'Getting pronoun badges right: Five recommendations for event organizers.' Medium, 4 September. Accessed on 26/06/2020 at https://medium.com/trans-talk/getting-pronoun-badges-right-five-recommendations-for-event-organizers-5458116b2ffc.

22 Pink Therapy Directory, www.pinktherapy.com/en-gb/findatherapist.aspx.

23 Miller, P.R., Flores, A.R., Haider-Markel, D.P., Lewis, D.C., Tadlock, B. and Taylor, J.K. (2020) 'The politics of being "Cait": Caitlyn Jenner, transphobia, and parasocial contact effects on transgender-related political attitudes.' *American Politics Research*, March 2020. doi: 10.1177/1532673X20906460.

24 'Transphobia rife among UK employers as 1 in 3 won't hire a transgender person.' Crossland Employment Solicitors, 18 June 2018. Accessed on 26/06/2020 at www.crosslandsolicitors.com/site/hr-hub/transgender-discrimination-in-UK-workplaces.

25 Scottish Transgender Alliance (2008) *Transgender Experiences in Scotland*. Edinburgh: Scottish Transgender Alliance. Accessed on 26/06/2020 at www.scottishtrans.org/wp-content/uploads/2013/03/staexperiencessummary03082.pdf.

26 Lesbian, gay, bisexual, transgender, queer (or questioning); the + is meant to cover members of sexual or gender minorities not explicitly included in the acronym.

27 Pharmaceutical Services Negotiating Committee (2020) 'Essential facts, stats and quotes relating to carers and providing carer support services.' Accessed on 26/06/2020 at https://psnc.org.uk/services-commissioning/essential-facts-stats-and-quotes-relating-to-carers-and-providing-carer-support-services.

28 Action on Hearing Loss, *Caring for Older People with Hearing Loss*. Accessed on 28/07/2020 at https://actiononhearingloss.org.uk/information-and-support/support-for-health-and-social-care-professionals/communication-tips-for-healthcare-professionals.

29 Royal National Institute of Blind People (RNIB) (2019) 'Key information and statistics on sight loss in the UK.' Accessed on 26/06/2020 at www.rnib.org.uk/knowledge-and-research-hub/key-information-and-statistics.

30 Weinstein, B.E. and Ventry, I.M. (1982) 'Hearing impairment and social isolation in the elderly.' *Journal of Speech and Hearing Research 25*, 593–599.

31 In practice, it is extremely rare for such exceptions to be granted.

32 Stonewall (2017) *LGBT in Britain: Hate Crime and Discrimination*. London: Stonewall, p.26. Accessed on 26/06/2020 at www.stonewall.org.uk/system/files/lgbt_in_britain_hate_crime.pdf.

33 Oral History Society (n.d.) 'LGBTQ: Lesbian, Gay, Bisexual, Transgender and Queer Special Interest Group.' Accessed on 26/06/2020 at www.ohs.org.uk/about/introducing-special-interest-groups/lgbtq.

34 This applies in England, Wales and Northern Ireland; the equivalent office in Scotland is the Procurator Fiscal.

Index

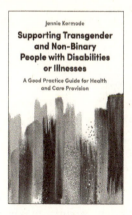

Supporting Transgender and Non-Binary People with Disabilities or Illnesses
A Good Practice Guide for Health and Care Provision
Jennie Kermode

£19.99 | $27.95 | PB | 184PP |
ISBN 978 1 78592 541 2 |
eISBN 978 1 78450 935 4

By drawing on the experience of trans people who are affected by physical disability, chronic illness and mental illness, this book is the definitive guide on providing best practice in approaches to health and care policy.

Suggesting solutions to areas where understanding and care provision are poor, Kermode gives advice on topics such as transitioning with a disability, sex-specific service provision and fertility and reproduction. The book also examines how health and care professionals can adapt to cater for transgender and non-binary people's needs and can support those who must use health services due to their condition.

Written in an accessible and comprehensive manner, *Supporting Transgender and Non-Binary People with Disabilities or Illnesses* is an essential guide for practitioners in health and social care positions.

Transgender Employees in the Workplace
A Guide for Employers
Jennie Kermode

£18.99 | $27.95 | PB | 216PP |
ISBN 978 1 78592 228 2 |
eISBN 978 1 78450 544 8

Respect and understanding between colleagues are essential in any healthy, productive, equal-opportunities workplace. But as an employer, are you aware of the specific needs of transgender employees and applicants?

This concise volume is the essential introduction for any employer on how to work effectively and respectfully with transgender employees, without asking the employee inappropriate or personal questions. In simple terms, it explains what it means to be transgender, the common challenges transgender people experience, and how you can best support transgender employees in their roles, and in their relationships with colleagues and clients.

The book clarifies employers' legal responsibilities towards employees, offers practical solutions to bullying, and provides information on health and safety as well as medical issues such as surgeries and hormone therapy. The glossary of terms elucidates the finer points, such as the correct language to use with the employee, and the crucial differences between transgender identities, including gender variant and non-binary. By improving professional relationships company-wide and promoting your employees' wellbeing, this book will ultimately assist you in building a happier and higher-performing work force.